GW01057501

SPIRITUAL FORCES IN INTERNATIONAL POLITICS

By the same author

CLIMAX OF HISTORY
MIDDLE EAST PERSPECTIVE
RUIN AND RESURGENCE: EUROPE 1939-1965
CREATING THE EUROPEAN COMMUNITY
DECLINE AND RENEWAL: EUROPE ANCIENT AND MODERN
MODERN PROPHETIC VOICES

SPIRITUAL FORCES IN INTERNATIONAL POLITICS

R.C. MOWAT

NEW CHERWELL PRESS • OXFORD

First published in Great Britain in 1998
by New Cherwell Press
7 Mount Street, Oxford OX2 6DH
Copyright © 1998 R.C. Mowat

ISBN: 1 900312 25 5

Cover Design by Philip Carr
Printed by Biddles, Guildford

PREFACE

I would like to say how grateful I am to all those who encouraged me in the writing of this book and in making earlier studies from which I drew much of my material. Three of these friends are sadly no longer with us, Michael Hutchinson, Bill Conner and Alwyn McKay. Others are too numerous to mention, though a special word should go to my son David for patiently teaching me how to use the computer and helping me through the fairly frequent occasions when I was stuck in operating it; also for processing and publishing the book by way of New Cherwell Press. And equally my warmest thanks and the dedication of the book go to Renée, my wife, for her unfailing support and care for my well-being.

Those who have read one or another of my former writings may find some passages having a familiar resonance. I admit to having shamelessly plagiarised from myself, especially from *Decline and Renewal* and *Modern Prophetic Voices*. My apologies for taking the liberty of this literary short-cut.

RCM.

CONTENTS

Appendices

INTRODUCTION

Martin Wight and I were exact contemporaries at Hertford College, Oxford in the early thirties. At that time we were both moving towards decisions concerning our respective philosophies of life, and it was natural that he became a confidant of my aspirations and difficulties. Our ways however parted. For many years when I was overseas there was little opportunity of meeting. My last recollection of him is lunching together at the London School of Economics. Any further chance of meeting again unfortunately disappeared with his early death in 1972 when he was still in his prime.

His International Relations classic, *Power Politics,* grew out of his Chatham House essay of 1946, followed by a posthumous edited version of a lecture series under the title *International Theory, the Three Traditions* (1991). These traditions are the Realist, the Rationalist and the Revolutionist, but he also discusses a fourth tradition which he calls 'inverted Revolutionism', the goal of which is 'evoking the latent power of love in all people, and transforming the world by the transformation of souls ... It is 'inverted' because it repudiates the use of power altogether; it is 'Revolutionist' because it sees this repudiation as a principle of universal validity, and energetically promotes its acceptance.'

In his early years Wight regarded Gandhi as the great contemporary exponent of these ideas. 'In Gandhi's evolution of satyagraha the Christian pacifist sees the rediscovery of the distinctively Christian technique of social and political activity, which revolutionised the Roman Empire in 300 years ... the organised application of the principles of the Sermon on the Mount.' Later, in defining the beliefs of the 'Inverted Revolutionists', he explained that 'they say, in effect, that the Sermon on the Mount lays down an absolute standard of ethics which is valid in all circumstances ... There is not a double standard of morality but a single one, and political ethics ought to be assimilated to private ethics.'

Though Wight's scepticism developed in later life, it must
have been the idealism of his Oxford days that brought us
together, since I shared such ideas. In my case these led me
towards the Oxford Group, known from 1938 onwards as Moral
Re-Armament (MRA). I later took part in its postwar conferences
at Caux in Switzerland — the subject of chapters 5 and 6 of this
book. These conferences are also the subject of the first case study
in *Religion, the Missing Dimension of Statecraft* by Douglas
Johnston and Cynthia Sampson. Along with other studies, these
supply the material for Johnston in calling for a new paradigm in
International Relations theory, based on the spiritual factor.

In his chapter 7 'International Revolutions' in *Power Politics*
Wight says that 'beliefs do not prevail in international politics
unless they are associated with power' (p.81), and adds that in
cases (Christianity being one of them) where this has happened,
they 'have gone through an important period before they captured
state power.' Following this line of thought I have attempted to
show how Christian ideology inspired a new approach to conflict
resolution after the fall of Nazism and Fascism, in the settlement
of Western Europe, whereby hereditary enemies were turned into
partners; also how, at that historic moment, these ideas — through
the dynamism and vision of the statesmen concerned — became
'associated with state power' and consequently prevailed. I also
survey the 'important' preliminary period which enabled this to
happen, through the training of those who set up and played the
major part in the Caux conferences which brought representatives
of the previously warring states together.

I have discussed this in chapter 8, for which I borrowed the
title of Johnston's book, as part of a wide-ranging survey of
spirituality as a prime element in shaping international relations,
with particular reference to the present critical period through
which we are living. Though the approach of the historian has to
be one of questioning (as well as questing), not without a tendency
to scepticism, I have not drifted into pessimism. I explore the

opportunities for maintaining Earth as a viable habitat for our descendants, and present the challenge to change if this is to be accomplished.

(Additional references: M.Wight: 'Christian Pacifism' in *Theology*, July 1936; *International Affairs*, April 1994, p.263, article by D.S.Yost.)

ACKNOWLEDGEMENTS

I am grateful to the authors and publishers on whose works I have been able to draw in using quotations: *The Times* (Lord Rees-Mogg and Dr. Alwyn McKay in Appendix 5 and Catherine Lucas in Appendix 6); also in the Appendices Dr. Charis Waddy, Michael Hutchinson (with permission of Mrs. Margaret Hutchinson), Dr Omnia Marzouk, Dr.André Chouraqui, Oxford University Press (quotations from R.C. Zaehner: *Hinduism*, about Mahatma Gandhi), and also on the same subject Rajmohan Gandhi: *The Good Boatman, a Portrait of Gandhi*, and Bharatiya Vidya Bhavan, Bombay: M.K. Gandhi: *The Message of Jesus Christ*; Princeton University Press and Dr. Walter Lowrie (quotations from *A Short Life of Kierkegaard*); Douglas Johnston and Cynthia Sampson: *Religion, the Missing Dimension of Statecraft;* Anne Wolrige Gordon: *Peter Howard, Life and Letters*; Susan Corcoran (letter from her father, Alan Thornhill); James Dale Davidson and Lord Rees-Mogg: *The Great Reckoning* and *The Sovereign Individual;* Professor Gertrude Himmelfarb: *The De-moralization of Society;* Professor J.K. Galbraith: *The Culture of Contentment;* Allan Griffith: *Peace-Building through the Ballot Box* (to be published); Leif Hovelsen: *Out of the Evil Night;* R.J. Hollingdale: translations from Nietzsche's *Twilight of the Idols and The Anti-Christ,* and *Thus Spoke Zarathustra*; Michael Henderson: *The Forgiveness Factor*; David J.H. Price: *Schuman, Acheson and supranationality,* and *The Moral Rearmament Movement and Postwar European Reconstruction.*

PLAN OF THE BOOK

I. POSITIVE AND NEGATIVE FORCES IN INTERNATIONAL RELATIONS

Chapter 1: Religion and reason of state. The postwar settlement in Western Europe as a new development in conflict resolution. Religion and 'reason of state' previously as factors in aggression. C15 Italy. Kant and the coming of a deeper Christianity relevant to international relations. Bismarck and von Gerlach. Britain's failure as honest broker in C19: racist nationalism and rapacity in the run-up to World War I.

Chapter 2: Approaches to history. Legendary or mythical history. Realism. Prophetic history: the Bible. State-centred history and 'complex interdependence': multinationals and revolutionary groups, spiritual and secular; positive and negative effects.

Chapter 3: Occultism in politics. Negative and destructive spirituality. Nietzsche: apparent influence on him of Oriental occultism by way of Helena Blavatskaya's theosophy. Immoralism. Transvaluation of values. Zarathustra. Impact of Nietzsche in Russia: Rasputin and the intelligentsia. End of Tsarism. Hitler, Himmler and occultism. The Nazi appropriation of Nietzsche.

II. POSTWAR PROBLEMS AND SOLUTIONS

Chapter 4: Leaders and their vision. Schuman, Adenauer, De Gasperi, Monnet. Need of 'prophetic' input: Buchman; Catholic and Protestant 'streams'.

Chapter 5: Conference with a new dimension. Caux postwar. Germans and French. Adenauer. Karl Arnold. Irène Laure. 'The forgiveness factor.' Labour-management relations. Directors of German coal-mines get together with French steel-masters − a step towards the European Coal and Steel Community.

Chapter 6: From conflict to partnership. The Ruhr as battle-ground between Communism and the West. Its centrality in moves towards the Community. André Philip and Schuman. Monnet and the Schuman Plan. Speed of making the Treaty of Paris and setting up the Community. A step towards realising Kant's vision.

Chapter 7: Ending civil war: Rhodesia and Zimbabwe. The part of three Christian 'streams', Quaker, MRA and Roman Catholic in ending civil war and creating Zimbabwe. The part of the Commonwealth. Alec Smith, Arthur Kanodereka, Lord Soames. Peacemaking through 'democratic legitimation'. Effect on Namibia and South Africa.

III. INTERNATIONAL RELATIONS IN THE INFORMATION AGE

Chapter 8: Religion, the Missing Dimension of Statecraft. Towards a new paradigm in International Relations, taking account of the spiritual factor and the part played by NGOs (Non-Governmental Organisations) in 'inspiring conflicting parties to move beyond the normal human reaction'. Theology and politics in first maintaining and then ending apartheid in South Africa. Religion and ethnic identity in ex-Yugoslavia. Interfaith dialogue and Track 2 diplomacy.

Chapter 9: The revolution of our time. The Information Revolution compared with the Agricultural Revolution which brought in civilisation. Has the nation-state a future? Has it a declining role in defence? China a future super-power? Mo-Ti (a successor of Confucius) and 'universal love'. 'The Sovereign Individual' and the rich/poor gap. 'The culture of contentment'. George Soros and international politics. A future for 'dynamic morality'? Retrospect: the end of the First Millennium.

Chapter 10: Streams of faith. The main streams of faith from the Renaissance/Reformation flowed together to provide the spiritual dynamic for the social and political changes which made possible the partnership of the previously warring states. Can these streams continue during the Information Revolution in such a way that it becomes a moral and spiritual revolution?

Chapter 11: Stop-go in spiritual progress. Spiritual 'streams' may flow for centuries, but the people whom they inspire are subject to the usual ups and downs in their experience and commitment. Great movements of faith initiate and mould cultures, but progress of such movements cannot be charted as a steadily rising graph. The pattern after the death or retirement of the initiator, as in the cases of the Franciscans, Quakers and Methodists, followed by revival with eventual achievements. MRA has apparently been going along the same lines, though there was a particularly dynamic phase during the leadership of Peter Howard.

IV. LOOKING TO THE FUTURE

Chapter 12: Preparing to act in the new dimension. This involves rigorous training such as that given by Buchman to the 'international team' in America before coming to Caux with them in 1946. The tough training he gave to Howard and which Howard gave to Alan Thornhill. Presenting the Cross in un-theological terms may be the central point of a new paradigm in International Relations.

Chapter 13: Action for the coming age. Conditions for operating in 'the new dimension of statecraft'. Continuity, each advance making possible the next, towards global transformation. Balkans and Bosnia. Interfaith developments.'Phase transitions' of adaptation at 'the edge of chaos'. 'Spontaneous organisation' as part of evolution. Design and purpose in the Universe. The creative minority. Six 'fundamental transitions' needed for global sustainability, including 'the renunciation or sublimation or transformation of our traditional appetites'. 'The butterfly effect'.

I: POSITIVE AND NEGATIVE SPIRITUAL FORCES IN INTERNATIONAL RELATIONS

CHAPTER 1

RELIGION AND REASON OF STATE

For any thinking person it is a commonplace that our species may be heading for disaster. The pollution of the environment, the squandering of resources, over-population and other abuses of the natural order may within a few generations make the habitat no longer viable. But there is at least one area where a legitimate hope may be cherished that there is a better way forward: mankind's means of resolving conflicts. For the first time in history, the aftermath of a major conflict – the second World War – saw not only the resumption of diplomatic relations between the contestants, but the formation of a partnership, on a basis that made it impossible for war to break out again between those states which entered into the arrangement.

Together these states, Western Germany, France, Italy, Belgium, the Netherlands and Luxembourg, made up a relatively small area of Europe, barely noticeable in a global map. Yet the step which they took may be a marking point in world history. The claim is a large one, and may be challenged by anyone living elsewhere than in the area concerned – for the geographical point where one is at the moment of thinking or writing, can largely determine one's perspective.

Indeed the period of recorded history shows other landmarks which, to contemporaries were similarly significant, for instance the creation of empires by figures who, at the time, appeared 'great' beyond the bounds of normal humanity: Ch'in Shih Hwang-ti in China, Sargon in the Middle East, Narmer in Egypt. In India Asoka, inspired by Buddhist teachings, abandoned his plan to complete the conquest of the sub-continent and publicly renounced war, devoting himself to spreading the doctrines of Gautama and providing for the welfare 'of all people'. As conqueror and creator of the Persian Empire, Cyrus refrained from coercion, encouraging exiles, such as the Jews at Babylon, to return to their cities and rebuild temples and houses. In Greece the

3

defeat of Xerxes was a similar marking moment, and for those inhabiting the area which became the Roman Empire there was something godlike about Augustus, as he established peace and order. In Arabia, the flight (Hegira) of Mohammed from Mecca to Medina in 622 CE opened a new era.

Until modern times religion always provided the motivation or the excuse for all kinds of political activity, often of aggressive intent. It inspired the incursion into Palestine and Syria of barbaric hordes from Western Europe as Crusaders, with murders and massacres en route and at Jerusalem, eventually wrecking the Byzantine Empire also. Another war was waged by Christians against Muslims in Spain, but there the reconquest had surprisingly good results. The new Archbishop of Toledo re-established (1125) the university there as a college of translators, many of whom were Christians and Jews as well as Muslims. In fact during three centuries in Spain there was a golden age when Muslims, Christians and Jews lived and worked together, creating the most brilliant civilisation of Medieval Europe. This remarkable achievement was ended by the bigotry and rapacity of Ferdinand and Isabella, who forced conversion or exile on their non-Christian subjects and conquered the flourishing emirate of Granada. Religion applied to politics had a similar adverse affect in Italy, when Sixtus IV (of Sistine Chapel fame) and succeeding Renaissance Popes used their position to extend the papal and family domains like any others among the rulers of Italy.[1]

Such misdirected applications of faith continued to motivate (or provide excuses for) the actions of those, whether Protestants or Catholics, who maintained the wars of religion, culminating in the partial wrecking of civilised life in Germany during the Thirty Years War. Thereafter religious excuses for aggression played less part as naked policies of rapacity took over, notably the seizure by the Prussian king, Frederick II ('the Great'), of Silesia from the inheritance of the Empress Maria Theresa of Austria. A few years later, in another act of cynical rapacity, Frederick joined with Maria Theresa and Catherine II (also 'the Great') of Russia in the first partition of Poland, which led a few years later to the rest of that country being shared among the same voracious neighbours. But as wars became more bloody through increasing fire-power and the total involvement of states with mass armies, the 'reason of state' approach began to be challenged. Frederick II could claim to be a new type of monarch, along with contemporaries like Catherine II, during the era in Europe known as 'the Enlightenment'. Christian scruples certainly went by the board with Frederick when it was a question of extending his territories, but the Christian leaven was still working in that era (approximately the 18th century) in Britain (the period of the Wesley brothers) and elsewhere. A deeper kind of faith, directly derived from the Gospels, was appearing as a challenge to rulers and governments.[2]

In the distant Prussian city of Königsberg (now Kaliningrad) the philosopher Immanuel Kant expressed his thought in the idioms of the day, which however do not obscure their Christian inspiration. Instead of 'God' he referred to 'Nature' or 'Providence' as the power educating mankind through wars 'which the depravity of human nature engendered'. Wars, he opined, are 'so many attempts to bring into being new relations among states'.[3] Ultimately 'reason tells them [states] to escape from the lawless condition of the savage: the way is to enter a federation in which even the smallest state can find safety'. In saying this Kant was thinking of Europe, though his words may suggest a wider application. In any case his Christian approach is evident when he asserts that such a new dispensation in the affairs of states could only take place if 'the last and most difficult step in human history' was to be achieved, 'the moralising of people. A long inner work in developing that secret essence in the education of its [the state's] citizens will be needed. Everything good that is not grafted on sound moral disposition is nothing other than meretricious show or glittering emptiness.'[4]

The work of Wesley, Wilberforce and their followers in the Evangelical Movement, along with Kierkegaard in Denmark, the Pietists in Germany, Lammenais, Gratry and others in France, had

5

laid the basis by the mid-19th century in Europe and America of the high Christian culture which flourished in the eighties and nineties, and continued until 1914. Statesmen of Christian conviction, like Gladstone, hoped that the 'Concert' of European states, originating from the war-time alliance against Napoleon and the Congress system which succeeded it, could resolve conflicts by consultation and diplomatic means. Part of this might be the acceptance of arbitration. The Russian initiatives in calling conferences at The Hague in 1899 and 1907 failed to bring about disarmament or obligatory arbitration, but they did result in setting up the Hague Arbitration Tribunal and later the International Court.

There were those in the Pietist tradition among the Prussian aristocracy who brought their convictions about conflict resolution into politics. One of these, Ludwig von Gerlach, tried but failed to win his friend Otto von Bismarck to these ideas. Bismarck had married into a family of Pietist convictions, and experienced something of a change. He became a Bible-reading Christian, abandoning the wild ways and dissipations of his younger years, but he kept this side of his life out of politics. For him 'reason of state' continued to prevail: to be swayed by any principles other than that of serving the interests of the state, no matter what one's personal predilections, smacked, in his view, of disloyalty to the ruler and country which one served. 'The function of religion in Bismarck's psychology,' writes one of his biographers, 'was to help him cope with the inner, purely personal problem created by the emotional starvation of his childhood. Religion gave him a sense of security.' But some elements of his personality remained the same. 'His need to dominate and direct did not spring from a sense of divine mission, but from an earlier, more elemental force in his personality ... His cynical view of minds and motives, his hatred and malevolence toward those who opposed him, his willingness to exploit and use others show that the Christian doctrine of love and charity had little influence upon him.'[5] Gerlach challenged his aggressive policies, warning him against 'the hideous and mistaken doctrine that God's holy ordinances do not apply to the sphere of politics, diplomacy and war ... as though these spheres were governed by no higher law than that of patriotic egoism.' But Bismarck 'brazenly denied any aggressive attitude.'[6] He broke off his friendship with Gerlach and secured his dismissal from his high judicial post.[7]

Bismarck rejected any belief such as Gladstone's that there was a divine order which was being progressively realised among men, and which, in Europe was to be perceived in the 'Concert'. Instead, with his wars against Denmark, Austria and France, he enlarged the sphere controlled by Prussia, converting it, along with the other German states, into the new German Empire (1871). During his last two decades of power he devoted himself to creating a system in which the new order would be maintained. But peace was not Bismarck's main objective. It was power, and this was what he bequeathed as his legacy. Misusing that power, his succesors engulfed Germany in two world wars.

Not that Germany alone was responsible for these disasters. Bismarck kept up an agitation during the early 1860's over the Duchies of Schleswig and Holstein, both under the Danish crown. Britain promised to stand by Denmark, but when the crisis arrived she let events take the course cunningly designed by Bismarck in collaboration with Austria. 'The course of events had brought it about that an agitation which had been begun [ostensibly] in order to secure the autonomy of the Duchies had ended by putting them under the heel of the Dual Alliance [of Prussia and Austria].' The diplomat Robert Morier, who had been working with the Foreign Secretary Lord John Russell during this period, said that 'when the casus foederis arose we abandoned like curs the country whose resistance to all compromise had been solely and entirely based on the belief that we should keep faith with her, and acknowledge the sacredness of engagements ... With the abandonment of Denmark began that decadence of our position and prestige in Europe.'[8]

Whether or not Bismarck might have been stopped in his tracks, he could at least have received a severe check, and Britain could have maintained her position as an honest broker helping to deal with the various international complications that were arising. Of these one of the most difficult to resolve was indeed the relation of Prussia to Austria and the German Confederation. The Prussian king wished to go slowly in this matter, as did Gerlach and others of the same persuasion, believing that this evolution was God-ordained, and should only take place by a thorough application of Christian principles. But Bismarck, on attaining power, was determined to force matters on, in order to create a Germany dominated by Prussia, for which its economic development and population growth gave it the strongest claim. Prussian initiative in the creation of the German Customs Union in 1834, with the gradual adherence of most other German states, had given it the strongest position in the resulting increase of trade and industry. With the political advantages that ensued there was the likelihood of unification being effected without strong-arm methods – though more slowly.

Kierkegaard's parable of the magnificent liner heading towards a white speck on the horizon, ignored by the captain and the cheerful company below decks, was being played out on a European scale.[9] The parable had been originally addressed to the Primate of Denmark, but Kierkegaard's concern was not only the clergy. The ordinary people were being fooled. 'There is a deceitful desire to avoid the truth that what is taking place with all the increasing millions ... is, from the Christian standpoint, a retrogression ... We have changed Christianity from a radical cure ... into a minor precaution, like something to prevent colds, toothache, and the like.'[10] Gerlach was in the position of the passenger in the parable, who tries to draw the captain's attention to the danger that is looming, but to no avail. 'It will be a dreadful night' – and so indeed it was, when a generation after Bismarck, the Great War came.

The militarist spirit in Germany resulting from the success of Bismarck's wars was such that it was difficult for her to broker the succession of critical situations in the Balkans resulting from the gradual rejection of Turkish rule. The Balkan wars of 1912 and 1913 had left a highly unstable situation when the assassination of the Archduke Franz Ferdinand at Sarajevo on 28 June 1914 triggered the crisis which needed all the arts of peacemaking if it was not to lead to catastrophe. This Germany was not able to supply — in fact her instigation of Austria to take a hard line with the Serbs was the immediate cause of the outbreak of war.

Of the other 'great powers' involved Britain was not in a position to work effectively with Germany for peace, even if the latter had desired it. An arrogant, even racist nationalism had begun to grip the British public as the 19th century ended. Whereas Gladstone was able to end the first South African (Boer) War by granting complete self-government to the Transvaal, events took a different turn as the second South African War (1899-1902) came on. The rapacity of Britons for gold and diamonds, 'buying land, digging mines, claiming citizenship'[11] in the Transvaal, was highly unsettling for the Afrikaner inhabitants (whatever the Africans themselves, regarded as politically negligible, may have thought). The flashpoint came with the raid of L.S. Jameson, an administrator of the trading Chartered Company recently set up by Britain, with 450 police. The war that followed was long and bloody by comparison with the first. Besides initiating concentration camps, it soured relations with Germany whose government had wished to show support for the Boers by sending a naval squadron to the nearest point on the coast — but British naval supremacy made this impracticable. This was the signal for Germany to start building a fleet which could rival Britain's, hence 'the naval race', a cause of ill-feelings between the two countries which contributed to the outbreak of war in 1914.

9

1."When Sixtus IV found no other object for the Papacy to pursue, he turned to the extension of the temporal power...The degradation of the Papacy had been gradual; in Alexander VI [Borgia] the Papacy stood forth in all its emancipation from morality...The Papacy no longer represented Christian morality in the international relations of Europe." - Mandell Creighton: *A History of the Papacy during the Period of the Reformation* (London 1887),IV:3,52.

2.See ch.10, especially pp.108*ff.*

3.I.Kant: *Perpetual Peace* (trans. M.Campbell Smith, London 1903),131,132.

4.I.Kant: *Idee einer allgemeiner Geschichte* in Kant's *Werke* (Leipzig 1838) VII,326,329.

5.Otto Pflanze: *Bismarck and the Development of Germany* (Princeton 1990),I,53.

6.Helmut Diwald (ed.): *Von der Revolution zum Norddeutschen Bund. Aus dem Nachlass von Ernst Ludwig von Gerlach,*Tagebuch 1848-1866 (Göttingen 1970),I,478-9.

7.Werner Richter: *Bismarck* (London 1964), 123,207. W.H.Simon: *Germany in the Age of Bismarck* (London 1958). Peter Hintzen: *Germany, a crucial chapter of Europe* (unpublished, trans. from *Duitsland - bewogen hart van Europa* (Sun, Nijmegen 1996).

8.R.B.Mowat: *A History of European Diplomacy 1815-1914* (London 1922),183.

9.H.V.HONG and E.H.Hong (editors): *Søren Kierkegaard's Journals and Papers* (Indiana University Press 1975), III,394-5

10.Ibid.,III,665,no.3612.

11.R.B.Mowat: *A New History of Great Britain* (Oxford 1926),941

CHAPTER 2

APPROACHES TO HISTORY

Events such as these can be narrated and interpreted in accordance with the standards set by 'The Peloponnesian War' of Thucydides in the fourth century BC. He wrote a dispassionate record of the facts, without legendary adornments or digressions. This may be called the realist approach, and is the standard way of writing history in modern times.

An earlier kind of history, both oral and literary, in all lands, is that of myth and legend. In Greek historical writing, long after Homer, myth and legend still linger, while they are the staple on which the tragedians based their plays. Later, in Rome, there is legend in Livy, while for Tacitus and Josephus history is 'realist'.

A third type of history is the prophetic. In the Bible there are myths of creation and other forms of poetry, together with legends of tribes with their wars and migrations, for the most part founded on fact. With Samuel 1 and 2 unadorned realism comes in, notably in dealing with the events of David's life and his numerous and obstreperous family. Legends do not seriously affect the basic historicity of the Gospels, particularly Mark,[1] while most of Acts — obviously the later part — are straightforward accounts of events in many of which Luke the writer participated. But in addition to realistic accounts in much of the Old as well as the New Testament, there is also interpretation of a prophetic kind.

This arises from the conviction that there is 'a divine purpose controlling all history and bringing it to its final goal',[2] and that within this purpose or plan there is a treaty or covenant which God made with the Israelites, whereby he assured them of his care and safekeeping as long as they walked in his ways, that is according to the moral law of the Ten Commandments and their later extension with 'love your neighbour as yourself'. Even more challenging 'is the far more significant and strenuous command: 'You shall not oppress the stranger ... instead you shall love him as yourself, for you were once strangers in the land of Egypt'.[3]

11

In the Bible the tragic element in prophecy often dominates. The prophet had to chastise his people with pictures of disaster that threatened because of their failure to keep their part of the covenant with God — while still pointing out that change would bring them to new life of fulfilment and happiness, when swords would be turned into ploughshares and 'they shall sit every man under his vine and under his fig tree, and none shall make them afraid ... For all people will walk every one in the name of his god, and we will walk in the name of the Lord our God for ever and ever.'[4] And there were what seemed miraculous interventions by the Almighty, at times of national crisis or prolonged difficulties, such as enabled Moses to lead the people from captivity in Egypt through the Red Sea towards the promised land. Another such miraculous event was Cyrus encouraging the Jews to return to Jerusalem from exile in Babylon.

Today the prophetic interpretation of history is as valid as in the days of the Hebrew prophets and Jesus. In his day the challenge to change went so far as not only to love the neighbour and stranger, but even the *enemy* (politically the Roman occupiers), otherwise disaster would overcome people, City and Temple. The 'powers of darkness' were waiting to do their evil work — as in the event they did within a generation of the rejection and crucifixion of Jesus. After a three-year siege the Romans captured Jerusalem, destroying the Temple and driving out most of the people.[5]

A 'realist' historian usually takes the state as the main agent. Hans Morgenthau sees the state as the human being writ large, with similar motives, 'to live, propagate, dominate.'[6] The perspective is determined by the place where the person is writing and also by the time. Thucydides was writing when the Greek states were in the last phase of their period of conflict, which took the form of the two leading states, Athens and Sparta, each with their satellites and allies, battling it out and so weakening themselves that all the combatants became ripe for take-over by a power on the fringe of their civilisation, Macedon. Morgenthau in America was writing at the time when the European states system was likewise giving way to the American hegemony. Such an evolution seems a normal historical development. China had also lived through its period of 'warring states' before they became part of Ch'in Shih Hwang-ti's empire. So with the former 'great powers' of Europe. When their two 'world wars' ended, Russia (as the Soviet Union) took over Central Europe while the rest came under the hegemony of America.

With the growing 'complex interdependence'[7]of states the challenge to historians is to focus less on writing state-centred history. 'There are actors other than states which play a central role in international events, the obvious examples being multi-national corporations and revolutionary groups.'[8] Multinationals were transferring certain powers of control away from the state. In Western Europe the increasing degree of interdependence reached a new level with the Community of Coal and Steel (later the EEC, then EU), merging the coalmining of the Ruhr with the steel-making of Lorraine. Federation, which was the ultimate aim of its creators, would take even more sovereign power away from the participating states.

As for 'revolutionary groups' some were spiritual, others secular. These could have a powerful impact, culturally progressive or destructive and cataclysmic. Some groups — such as the 'creative minorities' around Wesley, Wilberforce and other promoters of the British evangelical revival — have a positive impact on politics and society, even revolutionary over a period of decades. Others — Marxism, Nazism and occultism — prove revolutionary in a negative sense.

When occultism plays a prominent role the naked face of evil is shown, and disaster follows. The triumph of barefaced evil is preceded by a whittling away of moral standards in private and public life, and by a perverse application of principles such as underlay 'reason of state'.

The concept of sin is unfashionable, but private sin, such as selfishness, greed, perversion or adultery, can soon have an effect in the public domain, and unless taken seriously by a dynamic minority who accept self-discipline and sacrifice, will open the way for dramatic expressions of evil: rapacious materialism and misguided policies which bring disaster on a national or even world-wide scale.

Assuming there is a power of evil at work in the world, it does not take much imagination to see that the development of the high Judeo-Christian culture of the late 19th century in the West would be a target for its nihilistic efforts. Personal sins, including power-seeking and racial and other forms of superiority, fuelled national policies of rivalry and conflict, in particular between Germany and Britain, two nations which had so much in common and so many affinities, not to mention strong links through marriages, notably on the dynastic level. In finance and economic progress, in which Germany was forging ahead, there were strong reasons for maintaining a system which benefited not only the two countries chiefly concerned, but Europe and indeed the world as a whole. Viewed in this perspective, starting not only one but two wars in which Britain and Germany were the main antagonists at their inception, was a major coup by the evil forces.

But the powers of evil do not have it all their own way. In fact their existence and action are only comprehensible as being dependent on the powers of good, in Abrahamic terms of God. 'Death could not exist unless there were life, nor disease if there were no such thing as health ... Good might exist without evil, evil could not exist without good; for evil is either a parody of, or an obstacle to good.'[9] Even in the most desperate situation an extreme of evil can be overcome by an extreme of good.[10]

1.'Notwithstanding all the redactional and editorial manipulation carried out by the primitive church and the evangelists, a concrete basis exists on which to reconstruct history.' - Geza Vermes: *The Gospel of Jesus the Jew* (Riddell Memorial Lectures, University of Newcastle upon Tyne,1981),8; also *Jesus the Jew* (Collins, London 1973;Fontana 1976).

2.H. Wheeler Robinson: 'The Religion of Israel' in T.W.Manson (ed): *A Companion to the Bible* (Edinburgh 1939),290.

3.Jonathan Sacks: *The Politics of Hope* (London 1997),62. The distinction between 'covenant' and 'contract' follows,63. The quotations are from Leviticus 19,verses 18,34.

4.Micah 4: 3,4,5.

5.For further points on Rome and the destruction of Jerusalem see Appendix 4.

6.Hans J. Morgenthau: *Politics among Nations, the Struggle for Power and Place* (3rd edition, New York 1962),33.

7.Joseph S.Nye: *Understanding International Conflicts* (New York 1993),175.

8.Martin Hollis and Steve Smith: *Explaining and Understanding International Conflicts* (Oxford 1991),34.

9.Burnett Hillman Streeter: *Reality* (London 1927),222. Streeter (1874-1937) was well-known as a Biblical scholar and philosopher, Canon of Hereford 1915-1934 and Provost of the Queen's College, Oxford, from 1933. Among others of his books were *The Four Gospels, The Primitive Church, The Buddha and the Christ, The God who Speaks.*

10.Frank N.D.Buchman: *Remaking the World* (London 1961),162.

CHAPTER 3

OCCULTISM IN POLITICS

By the turn of the century Marx's thought had established itself in intellectual circles and left-wing politics. Another potent influence was that of Nietzsche, shortly to be followed by Freud and Einstein. Relativity is a scientfic concept, but when construed in a general way 'the belief began to circulate ... at a popular level [in the 1920's] that there were no longer any absolutes, [cutting] society adrift from its traditional moorings in the faith and morals of Judaeo-Christian culture[1] ... Artists, philosophers and scientists were nibbling and hacking away at the absolute standards of the old confident West.'[2]

The view of the innovating sociologist, Max Weber, early in the century, was that 'our intellectual universe has largely been formed by Marx and Nietzsche.'[3] Marx proclaimed what he believed to be the scientific laws which governed the processes of historical change, and which were as certain and regular as the scientific laws which, according to Newton, governed the functioning of the universe. 'True insight into the nature and laws of the historical process will of itself, without the aid of independently known moral standards ... indicate the form of life which it is rational to pursue.'[4] By contrast with this highly intellectual approach, Nietzsche offered spiritual fare – but nonetheless revolutionary.

> His 'transvaluation of values' was to be the final, ultimate revolution, a revolution against both the classical virtues and the Judaic-Christian ones. The 'death of God' would mean the death of morality and the death of truth – above all, the truth of any morality. There would be no good and evil, no virtue and no vice. There would be only 'values'. And having degraded virtues into values, Nietzsche proceeded to de-value and trans-value them, to create a new set of values for his 'new man'.[5]

16

Part of the appeal of Marx and Nietzsche was that they both offered new non-Christian understanding of the oncoming decadence and what to do about it, while powerful resonances remained in their writings of the Judaeo-Christian faith that permeated the existing culture. Marx was brought up in a Jewish family. Nietzsche, though having a father and both grandfathers who were Lutheran ministers, lost his faith. Marx wrote as an Old Testament prophet about the coming age, assuming humanity would escape from 'the common ruin of the contending classes'.[6] Nietzsche's original inspiration was the New Testament. Both looked to the coming of a new order of society with a new type of human. In Marx it was to be the worker liberated from class oppression. With Nietzsche it was the superman, the man who would overcome himself.

Nietzsche's 'earliest ideas ... now came up transformed and distorted almost beyond recognition.'[7] In the person of Zarathustra he sees himself called to be the leaven in the world's lump. 'You have lain like leavened dough, your soul has risen and overflowed its brim ... Every soul is a world of its own[8] ... Heal your soul with new songs so that you may bear your great destiny, that never yet was the destiny of any man ... You are the teacher of the eternal recurrence, that is now your destiny ... I am part of the eternal recurrence ... to speak once more the teaching of the great noon-tide of earth and man, to tell man of the Superman once more.'

What is wrong with human society, says Nietzsche, is 'decadence' — the product of 'an 'altruistic' morality under which egoism *languishes* ... Man is finished when he becomes altruistic ... Everything *good* is instinct — and consequently easy, necessary, free ... We immoralists especially are trying with all our might to remove the concept of guilt.' When instinct is allowed its proper role a person can become 'Dionysian' — 'the entire emotional system is alerted and intensified.' He deplores the 'barren spirituality, grown how centred and lukewarm!' in the German

17

universities of his day.[9]

It is in dealing with Jesus that Nietzsche cannot wholly escape from his inherited convictions. He recognises his heroic traits, sharply differentiating him from Christianity. 'I confess,' he says, 'there are few books which present me with so many difficulties as the Gospels do.' But 'to make a hero of Jesus!' – he jibs at that. Nonetheless that is practically what he does, and in doing so he says some interesting things, for instance 'the 'kingdom of Heaven' is a condition of the heart – not something that comes 'upon the earth' or 'after death' ... [It] is not something one waits for; it has no yesterday or tomorrow, it does not come "in a thousand years" – it is an experience within a heart; it is everywhere, it is nowhere.' Jesus 'died as he lived, as he taught – not to 'redeem mankind' but to demonstrate how one ought to live.'[10]

Apparently Nietzsche was strongly influenced by theosophy, knowledge of which was becoming available to Western intellectuals through the the work of Mme. Blavatsky (more correctly Blavatskaya), especially through her two-volume book, *Isis Unveiled*, published in New York in 1877. Née Helena von Hahn – she had grandparents who had migrated from Germany to Russia – and endowed with extraordinary psychic powers, she travelled, after a brief marriage, in India and the borders of Tibet. She met a retired British officer, Col.H.S. Olcott, in 1873: they founded Theosophical Societies first in India, then in New York (1875), with branches in Paris, London (1878), and elsewhere – and a magazine, 'Theosophist'. London became her home, with visits to Germany and Belgium, until her death in 1891.[11] There are many echoes of theosophy in *Thus Spoke Zarathustra* (1883) and other books of Nietzsche's last decade before he was certified insane and ceased writing in 1889.

This modern version of ancient Gnosticism aims at penetrating to the knowledge (*gnosis*) of religions and spiritual experiences in general, all of which are 'but shoots and branches [which] spring from the same trunk.' This Wisdom Religion has been preserved 'among initiates in every country', especially India, Central Asia and Iran.[12] There are 'occult lodges throughout the world, ranging from the white through all shades of grey to black[13] ... Occultists who are unselfish and wholly devoted to the carrying out of the Divine Will are called "white". Those who are selfish and are working against the Divine purpose in the universe are called "black". The "Black Path" leads to gaining control of "elementals" or "nature-spirits" ... a mighty host ... At the head of each division is a great Being, the directing and guiding intelligence of a whole department of nature ... Occult qualities or supernatural powers, as alchemy, magic, necromancy, are real, actual and very dangerous sciences.[14] Nature-spirits ... most frequently of all terrestrial elementary spirits [are] disembodied evil men.'

In personal life occultism may bring disasters. 'Many happy homes have been broken up as a result of the teaching of spirits, that everyone has a twin soul. The spirits even go so far as to introduce "twin-souls" to each other, after which introductions they are encouraged to leave homes, husbands, wives and children, to live together.'[15]

How much did Nietzsche dabble in this kind of occultism? He was led into it by his interest in Buddhism, which (in his view) is 'a hundred times more realistic than Christianity. It arrives *after* a philosophical movement lasting hundreds of years; the concept 'God' is already abolished by the time it arrives ... It no longer speaks of 'the struggle against *sin*' but ... 'the struggle against *suffering*' ... It stands in my language, *beyond good and evil*.'[16]

In the thousand pages of *Isis Unveiled*, Blavatsky claims to present 'the ancient universal Wisdom Religion as the only possible key to the Absolute in science and theology.' She explains how 'the immortal spirit' enters into man, and 'pervading his whole being makes of him a god, [like] Zarathustra and his followers, the Zoroastrians ... All these gods [are] *occult powers*

19

of nature.'[17] The question arises as to whether Nietzsche, taking on himself the role of a prophet, believed himself to be a reincarnation of Zarathustra (Zoroaster), preaching the imminence of the great noon-tide or the eternal return – 'a certain period of cosmical activity', in Blavatsky's words, and 'an equal one of cosmical repose.'[18]

Nietzsche's thought is similar to that of modern 'New Age'occultism where the morality of the Abrahamic faiths has disappeared – everything is one, including good and evil, ourselves and God. The build-up of self to becoming superman is part of being God: 'the individual self or soul is the universal self or soul.'[19] In Britain the Findhorn conference centre provides courses in all aspects of New Ageism. It has been called 'the Vatican city of the New Age movement'.[20]

Societies which are in psychological trouble are attacked by the powers of evil: occultism; erotic and violent ideologies; murders and massacres; the ravages of drink and drugs. In Russia, as far back as the 1870s the educated elite – the intelligentsia – had turned against the monarchy after the brutal suppression of the 'going to the people' movement of the students. Lord Radstock's evangelical movement, directed to the aristocracy, with far-reaching repercussions among students and (in some regions) even among the peasantry, might have given another chance for Tsar and intelligentsia to find enough unity to move together with policies of reform and regeneration. But Tsar Alexander II had been obliged to expel Radstock,[21] and his followers were suppressed. In spite of the abolition of serfdom by Alexander, and the later reforms of peasant landholding by Stolypin, with boom conditions in the small but growing industrial sector in the first years of the 20th century, the psychological and moral situation was becoming desperate.

There is no need to elaborate on the part of Marxism in shaping the culture and politics of the 20th century, notably the disastrous effects in its Leninist form on Russia and other countries. The influence of Nietzsche may not be so obvious, but it was already penetrating intellectual circles in Russia as the 19th century ended. Many young men and women, especially some of the most promising, were attracted, and sometimes captured for life, by the ideologies of Marx or Nietzsche. Some who saw through, or were immune to the doctrines of both, became members of the brilliant group who took part in 'the Russian religious renaissance of the 20th century',[22] cut short by the Bolshevik regime. Whatever the influences, occultism in Russia as the century ended was beginning to show its nefarious 'Black Path' power both in culture and politics.

Its most notorious practitioner was Rasputin, introduced into the family circle of Tsar Nicholas II by a well-meaning cleric who was confessor to the imperial couple. Rasputin became a fixture there owing to his hypnotic power of healing the illnesses of the haemophiliac young heir to the throne, which brought him into the good graces of the somewhat unbalanced, mystically minded Empress.

Rasputin was an uneducated peasant who 'belonged to the religious underworld concealed beneath the stately structure of Russian Orthodoxy ... He shared the teaching of the Khlysty, an orgiastic sect, according to which the soul of a man "possessed by the Holy Ghost" could not be polluted by any carnal transgression' – and these, in the case of Rasputin, were habitual and frequent. They were concealed from the Empress, while her husband was too weak to proceed against him. The intimate friend of the Empress (practically the only one), Ana Vyrubova,[23] provided a permanent link by telephone from her apartment in the palace grounds. As the power of the Tsar dwindled when he left St.Petersburg to direct operations at headquarters during the war, Rasputin, Vyrubova and the Empress virtually took over running the country – to complete disaster, culminating in the Bolshevik seizure of power and the massacre of the imperial family.[24]

Rasputin 'symbolized the confusion and corruption of the era ... The ruling class of Russia had insufficient moral stamina to resist effectively the pernicious influence of the immoral mystic.[25][His] orgies, intermingled with his religious performances, were only the extreme and crudest expressions of the unhealthy state into which many Russians had sunk.'[26]

Nietzsche's 'ferocious onslaught upon the pseudo-values of mass culture ... found an immediate echo in Russian minds.' Russians 'were fascinated — both attracted and repelled — by those passages in *Thus Spoke Zarathustra* ... which explicitly and harshly repudiated 'love of one's neighbour''.[27] His influence in Russia was 'profound, widespread and enduring.'[28] Valery Bryusov's books popularised black magic and eroticism, with his doctrine that there was no distinction between good and evil (he was one of the first writers to welcome the Bolshevik victory). V.V. Rozanov's beliefs were similar — he worshipped an unknown god. Alexander Blok was an anti-Christian mystic. Some poets were prophesying a 'superman' — their writings were 'a mixture of eroticism, cynicism and despair.'[29]

Today occultism is said to be widespread in the former Soviet Union.[30]

In Germany the shock and frustration of losing the war, aggravated by the punitive peace imposed at Versailles, was followed a few years later by the misery resulting from the French re-occupation of the Ruhr and the subsequent hyper-inflation. The 'incalculable depths into which Germany had fallen'[31] returned again after the brief recovery of the late 20s, when the Wall Street crash signalled deflationary policies and mass unemployment in Germany and elsewhere. Hitler rose to power on the hopes by many for national regeneration, in the demoralising twilight days of the Weimar regime.

Nietzsche's influence and the political power of occultism were revealed in the Nazi regime, although there is no clear direct link between Nietzsche's teaching and the kind of occultism which Hitler absorbed in Vienna in the years before 1914. The drab under-world of Vienna, into which Hitler sank after his failure to secure a place at the Academy of Fine Arts, was a breeding-ground of virulent anti-semitism linked with Pan-Germanic visions and occultist mythology, propagated notably by the review 'Ostara' of which Hitler was a regular reader.[32]

Hitler volunteered for service in the German army in 1914, and towards the end of his time found himself in the education and propaganda section at Munich. There he became a member of the German Workers National Socialist Party (NSDAP) – the germ of the mass organisation with which he eventually took power, but at that time (1919) a small group which had been infiltrated by the occultist Thule Society. A moving spirit in the Thule Munich Lodge was Karl Haushofer, Professor of Geopolitics ('space is power') at the university. During travels in Central Asia Haushofer had discovered a region which he believed to be the mythical Thule, the original homeland of the Aryans or 'Germanen'.[33] One of his most assiduous students was the ex-service Luftwaffe pilot, Rudolf Hess, who became his 'Scientific Assistant'.[34]

Through the NSDAP Hitler came to know him and Haushofer. After his failed coup (1923) when he was in the Landsberg Prison, Hess and Haushofer spent long hours with him (in this modern gaol Hitler had a two-room suite and the opportunity to entertain his friends). He underwent a kind of conversion, accepting the occultist doctrine that a new 'spiritual millennium' was beginning. Encouraged by these friends and others, Hitler saw himself as the destined leader endowed with all powers needed to bring the nations into subjection. Those who knew him recognised the change in him after his Landsberg experience. Resuming his political activity on his release, his speeches, prepared by trance-like communings with occult forces, came forth with a torrent of words, received by many as inspired.

Coming by a different route, Himmler practised another, but no less deadly, type of occultism. He literally worshipped the spirit of the early medieval Emperor Henry II, conqueror of the Slavs, annually spending hours at his tomb, whence he received psychic power, with apparitions of his hero. After the Nazis took over the

23

government and started concentration camps, it became possible for him to use the victims as slave-labour for rebuilding the ruined Wewelsburg Castle as the centre of the Black Order – his revival, in a new version, of the Teutonic Knights who had won East Prussia from the Slavs. Wewelsburg was also a shrine for the elite SS of the Order: sombre rituals were performed echoing Himmler's inherited (but rejected) Catholicism, blended with Germanic paganism.

The Nazis were not just copying Christian rites when they staged the Party Days at Nuremberg with grandiose ceremonies, turning the stadium into a kind of cathedral -they were the rites appropriate for their perverted form of faith. The word 'Reich' had religious connotations, harking back to medieval concepts. Their Reich had its martyrs, notably the sixteen dead in Hitler's 1923 coup, for whom twice-yearly memorial services were staged which would have done honour to the saints. Its millenarian prospects – the Reich of a thousand years – would fufill the prophecies of old. Hitler was both High Priest and Saviour, sent by 'Providence' to accomplish the destiny of the Aryan race – all others would bow down or be destroyed.

As the Nazis moved towards power, and particularly after attaining it, Nietzsche was appropriated by them. There was much in his writings to enable them to claim him as their prophet, foreseeing their role as 'Aryan humanity, quite pure, quite primordial', whereas Christianity represented 'the *reaction* against the morality of breeding, of race, of privilege – it is the *anti-Aryan* religion *par excellence.*'[35] But 'our way is upward, from the species across to the super-species. You could surely create the Superman[36] ... and Caesarian spirits might also be produced ... This new race would climb aloft to new and hitherto impossible things, to a broader vision, and to its task on earth.'[37] But like so much of Nietzsche's writings, there are many contradictions, pro-Prussian and anti-German, pro-Jew and antisemitic – there were many difficulties for the Nazi expositors, but they brushed them

24

aside, or cut offending passages from their texts.

1.Paul Johnson: *A History of the Modern World* (London 1983),4,5.
2.J.M.Roberts: *The Triumph of the West* (London 1985),11.
3.Gertrude Himmelfarb: *The De-moralisation of Society* (New York 1994),11.
4.Isaiah Berlin: *Karl Marx* (Oxford 1963),6,7.
5.Gertrude Himmelfarb: *The De-moralization of Society, from Victorian Virtues to Modern Values* (New York 1995),10.
6.*The Communist Manifesto.*
7.Nietzsche: *Thus Spoke Zarathustra* (Trans. with Introduction, R.J. Hollingdale, Harmondsworth 1969),28 (Introduction).
8.Ibid.,234,237,238.
9.Nietzsche: *Twilight of the Idols* and *The Anti-Christ* (trans. with Introduction and Commentary R.J.Hollingdale, Harmondsworth 1968),T.87,48,53,73,61.
10.Ibid.(Anti): 140,141,146,147.
11.Herbert Whyte: *H.P.Blavatsky* (London 1909). A.P.Sinnett: *Incidents in the Life of Mme.Blavatsky* (London 1886). Sinnett also wrote *Esoteric Buddhism.* Pamphlets, e.g.'The Ladies' Theosophical Society', with 'Hints on esoteric theosophy' (Allahabad 1882).
12.Helena Blavatsky (Blavatskaya): *The Key to Theosophy* (London 1889),5.
13.Annie Besant: *The Ancient Wisdom* (London 1897),91.
14.Blavatsky,26.
15.Raphael Gasson: *The Challenging Counterfeit* (Bridge Publishing Inc.,Valley Books,Gwent 1985),52.
16.Nietzsche: *Anti-Christ* (op.cit.),129
17.*Isis Unveiled*,II,143.
18.Ibid,II,421.
19.David Marshall: *New Age vs.the Gospel* (Autumn House, Alma Park,Grantham 1993), 1,74,85.

20.Ibid.,85.

21.See Appendix 1.

22.Nicholas Zernov: *The Russian Religious Renaissance of the Twentieth Century* (London 1963),168; Philip Boobbyer: *S.L.Frank, The Life and Work of a Russian Philosopher* (Ohio University Press 1995),60*ff.*

23.Ana Vyrubova: *The Romanov Family Album* (Vendome Press,New York 1982),19ff.

24.M.V.Rodzianko: *The Reign of Rasputin* (tr.Zvegintzoff,London 1927).

25.Zernov,op.cit.,173.

26.Ibid.,178.

27.Bernice Rosenthal (ed.): *Nietzsche in Russia* (Princeton 1986), foreword by George L.Kline,xii.

28.Ibid.(Rosenthal),3.

29.Zernov,176.

30.Information from Lawrence Uzzell, Keston Institute,31/10/96.

31.Vera Brittain: *Testament of Youth* (London 1992),645.

32.Nicholas Goodrick-Clarke: *The Occult Roots of Nazism* (Tauris,London 1992),198. See also René Alleau: *Hitler et les sociétés secrètes* (Paris 1969); Louis Pauwels et Jacques Bergier: *Le Matin des magiciens* (Paris 1960, Eng.trans.London 1971); André Brissaud: Hitler et l'ordre noir (Paris 1969); Werner Maser: *Der Frühgeschichte der NSDAP* (Frankfurt-am-Main 1965).

33.Karl Haushofer: *Deutsche Politik im indopazifischen Raum* (Hamburg 1939).

34.Alleau,op.cit. Further references in R.C. Mowat: *Decline and Renewal* (New Cherwell Press, Oxford 1991).

35.Nietzsche: *Twilight of the Idols,* op.cit.,92,93; *The Anti-Christ*,180.

36.Nietzsche: *Zarathustra,*100,110.

37.Crane Brinton: *Nietzsche* (New York 1965),213, cited from Nietzsche: *The Will to Power*,954.

II: POSTWAR PROBLEMS AND SOLUTIONS

CHAPTER 4

LEADERS AND THEIR VISION

An extreme of evil must be overcome by an extreme of good – a commitment to good on the part of the principal protagonists. During the second World War there were in fact people who had made remarkable sacrifices, who in many cases had been persecuted and had suffered, and who were now ready to step out on to the stage of history, replacing the dictators and their minions, in an action capable of changing the course of events on a global scale. Of these there were the statesmen, men of Christian conviction, able to act on the promptings of their faith for co-operation and the regeneration of their countries: Adenauer, Schuman, De Gasperi, all were dedicated Roman Catholics, survivors through two World Wars of the high Christian culture of the last decades before 1914. They were supported by Churchill and Truman (more particularly by his Secretaries of State, George Marshall and Dean Acheson), and owed much that was essential in their work to Jean Monnet.

In a 'Christian counter-attack' these leaders were prepared not only to forgive their enemies but to work together with them for a settlement which would outlaw war between their countries for ever. But to launch this policy there was the need for another factor, the prophetic kind, a type of moral and spiritual leadership which could mobilise people of every class and background, providing the inspiration and the popular backing for realising the best plans which the leadership could project.

This came in large measure from another representative of the former Christian culture, Frank Buchman, initiator of the Oxford Group which had moved into a world role as Moral Re-Armament. An ordained American Lutheran, descended from Swiss immigrants to Pennsylvania who, along with German settlers, had maintained their original language, he had a particular concern for, and a deep sense of commitment to Germany.

Robert Schuman, who was Prime Minister of France, 1947-8, then Minister for Foreign Affairs until 1953, followed Kant in believing that federation could bring the end of Europe's long succession of wars. But he realised that it was necessary to proceed by stages. The first step was to reintegrate Germany (apart from its eastern provinces under Soviet Russia) within Western Europe, and to do this 'by procedures such that the advance made on the road to federation is irreversible.'[1]

The condition for this was a change in public opinion at a time when Germans were widely regarded as pariahs. A man of vision, Schuman saw this change as part of a renewal of Christian culture, which should particularly include the younger generation. 'Wars have ravaged hearts and minds more ruinously than the material devastation,' he said. 'We need to imbue the youth of all countries with an ideal ... [the] values which made our Christian culture.'[2]

Frank Buchman expressed no particular views in respect of the future structure of Germany or of Europe when he arrived at Caux in July 1946, but like Schuman he was convinced that the new Europe could not be built without the Germans. Hence his question on arrival, which caused some consternation among those present, 'where are the Germans?' There followed the moves with the occupying authorities in Western Germany which brought the Germans to Caux. He also believed in renewing Christian culture as part of saving and remaking civilisation, though his vision carried him beyond Schuman's to 'remaking the world', and to doing this by changing individuals.

It was this vision, with the conviction that the way to realising it was through changing people, that made Buchman's approach different from that of the Churches. 'Changing human nature and remaking men and nations' was an alternative, and one much sounder, both philosophically and morally, to Communism, to which it presented the sole effective ideological challenge since the overthrow of Nazism. Though many members of the Churches, Catholic, Orthodox and Evangelical, rallied to Moral Re-Armament, the Churches themselves were not in the battle for building a new world. In contrast, Buchman and his co-workers not only realised that they were in a fight for the future of humanity, but they had a strategy for pursuing this end.

These convictions brought Schuman close to Buchman even before they met in 1948. They also held in common a view concerning the basis of European civilisation. As Schuman put it:

> Christ's kingdom was not of this world. That means also that Christian civilisation should not be the product of a violent and sudden revolution, but of a progressive transformation, of a patient education, under the action of the great principles of caring, of sacrifice and of humility, which are the foundations of the new society.[3]

The same thought is also found in the preface which he wrote for the French version of Buchman's speeches. Though he had not yet been to Caux, he understood clearly its purpose and approach.

> What we need, and what is quite new, is a school where, by a process of mutual teaching we can work out our practical behaviour towards others; a school where Christian principles are not only applied and proven in the relationships of man to man, but succeed in overcoming the prejudices and enmities which separate classes, races and nations ... To provide teams of trained men, ready for the service of the state, apostles of reconciliation and builders of a new world, that is the beginning of a far-reaching transformation of society in which, during fifteen war-ravaged years, the first steps have already been taken. It is not a question of a change of policy; it is a question of changing men. Democracy and her freedoms can be saved only by the quality of the men who speak in her name.[4]

With the other main architect of European unity, Jean Monnet, Buchman did not have the same personal touches, though in their vision and approach they had much in common. In Algiers with De Gaulle in 1943 Monnet had expressed his vision for a 'European entity' free of frontier-posts and tariff barriers, in which all the democratic liberties would be maintained, essential as the foundation of Western civilisation. He pointed out that peace could not be assured in Europe 'if the states were reconstituted on a basis of national sovereignty involving as it would policies of prestige and economic protection ... Prosperity and the indispensable social developments are impossible, unless the states of Europe form themselves into a federation or a "European entity"'.[5] Schuman, Monnet and Buchman all believed, in different ways, in seeking direction in their affairs in the early morning of each day. While Schuman sought his inspiration at Mass in the chapel opposite his house at Scy-Chazelles, Monnet's inspired hunches came to him during his morning walks, after which he would come to the office 'electrically charged with priorities and ideas which fell like hail on subordinates' desks.'[6] Though not a churchgoer, Monnet's upbringing in a Catholic home had left its mark on many aspects of his life, not least in this morning equivalent to what, for Buchman, was a 'quiet time'.

These habits of a life-time sustained all three men in their vision of revolutionary changes, and in suggesting the means for realising them by strategic action with a sure touch for timing. Although 'revolution' was not a word which Monnet used in connection with his work, the radical changes which he initiated were nothing less. 'We are starting a process of continuous reform' he said, 'which can shape tomorrow's world more lastingly than the principles of revolution so widespread outside the West'.[7] Also like Buchman he was a man who was equally at home in different countries besides his native France, notably in England and America, where – again like Buchman – he had many friends in 'those informal Washington networks' whose cooperation was essential at a period when the initiatives of both men, and of Schuman, could only succeed with the backing of the United States.[8] Along with these men, Konrad Adenauer, Chancellor of the (West) German Federal Republic and Alcide De Gasperi, the first Prime Minister of postwar Italy, are counted as initiators of the first European Community. The fact that, like Schuman, they were dedicated Catholics, might give the impression that unifying Western Europe was the realisation of a Catholic vision by Catholic statesmen. Indeed Cardinal Hume, writing in the Benedictine tradition, has said 'we dream of a Europe which will discover its faith and its unity, ... whose peoples will be free to inherit their own history and their identity.'[9]

Europe certainly owes much to its Roman Catholic core in Adenauer's Rhineland and Schuman's Lorraine, as also to De Gasperi's Tyrol − not forgetting that he was given sanctuary from Fascism by a job in the Vatican Library − and that the tradition of radical Catholicism coming down from Lamennais, Gratry and Sangnier to Schuman was one of the main 'streams' that converged at this time to supply the dynamic for creating the new Europe. But the other streams were Protestant: German Pietism in the tradition of Bonhoeffer and the Confessing Church which had stood out against Hitler, and the Anglo-American stream descending through Moody, Drummond, Mott and Buchman.

Frank Buchman's dynamism stemmed from his experience as a young man at the Keswick Convention in 1908.[10] He had come to Europe in a spirit of resentment, having resigned from being manager of a church hostel in Philadelphia after a quarrel with the supervisory committee about the quality and cost of food for the residents. Listening to a talk in a Keswick chapel he sudddenly 'had a poignant vision of the Crucified. There was infinite suffering on the face of the Master, and I realised for the first time the great abyss separating myself from Him. That was all. But it produced in me a vibrant feeling, as though a strong current of life had suddenly been poured into me, and afterwards a dazed sense of a great spiritual shaking-up ... A wave of strong emotion, following the will to surrender, rose up within me from the depths of an estranged spiritual life, and seemed to lift my soul from its anchorage of selfishness, bearing it across that great sundering abyss to the foot of the Cross.' He immediately wrote to the committee men, apologising for his resentment and asking their forgiveness.[11]

That afternoon a Cambridge man who had been brought to the Convention by his parents, struck by the change in Buchman, asked for a walk and talk. 'Before we returned he, too, decided to make the surrender of his will to Christ's will.'[12] Thereafter the spiritual dynamism which characterised Buchman was imparted to thousands of people round the world during the following decades. Much of his action took place at Oxford after the first World War, giving rise to the name Oxford Group.

After Hitler took power in Germany and another war began to loom, Buchman did not relax his efforts to bring the country back to finding its role under God in Europe and the world. But in 1936 he was rejected at an interview with Himmler. Himmler had been trying to swing the Group behind the Nazis. According to the account of a journalist whom Buchman saw immediately after the interview, it 'became a complete fiasco. Himmler could not, as he intended, exploit the 'absolute obedience' of the Group.' Buchman's conclusion was that 'Germany has come under the dominion of a terrible demoniac force,' and that some counter-action was urgently needed.[13]

This involved, among other things, intensive action in countries neighbouring Germany. Meanwhile the war, when it came, had to be won, and it was with this objective, as well as with the longer-term commitment to Germany and Europe, that Buchman in America undertook three months of training a hundred or more of his team in 1940 in a group of holiday cottages at Lake Tahoe. It was training in the household arts as part of a process whereby 'the rough corners of our human natures had to be rubbed off. The human preconceptions deriving from our backgrounds and nationalities had to be surrendered. Unity could not be bought at a lesser price than an honest facing of and restitution for all that brings divisions between man and man: dishonesty, impurity, selfishness and lack of love in all its forms – hatred, resentment, bitterness.'[14]

But together with the 'pain and tears' there was also much cheerfulness and merriment, when what became known as 'the floor show' developed into the 'new vehicle for the message' for which Buchman had been hoping – the first full-scale review put on by MRA, 'You can defend America', which with the accompanying handbook went throughout the United States.

Those whom Buchman had trained went on to provide the core of 'the international team' at the permanent centre at Mackinac, Michigan, where Island House, which had seen better days, was leased for a nominal rent, and became the venue for conferences at a time when practically no paid staff were available. 'Not only had Buchman managed to achieve through his training the teamwork he had envisioned long ago,' writes 'Bunny' Austin (a participant) 'but we were able to staff and run Island House ourselves ... The spirit in which Island House was run was a practical demonstration of MRA at work, adding vastly to the reality of the meetings held and the plays performed.'[15] This was the pattern and the spirit which, transplanted to Caux, enabled the European conferences to start in an equally effective way – 'the magic' of the atmosphere which enabled even the most unlikely people to make decisions which opened up new lives for themselves and those with whom they came into contact.

This spiritual and moral dynamism, for the time being at least, made the 'reason of state' approach to politics yield to a genuinely Christian way for transforming the situation. Long before Frederick the Great seized Silesia from Austria and after Bismarck had brought about his three victorious wars, reason of state had ruled as the mode of proceeding in international affairs. It had again been followed after the new German Empire's victory over France in 1871, and, when the tables turned, in the vindictive peace imposed by France and her allies in 1919. Now, with

Prussia under Soviet rule, the Federal Republic had nothing to lose by accepting that 'God's holy ordinances' (in the words of von Gerlach, Bismarck's challenger) should apply 'to the sphere of politics, diplomacy and war'. More important at the time was that France was ready to accept the same principle.

It was the breaking of the chain of fate. The Cold War was at its height − Czechoslovakia was taken into the Soviet empire in 1948 and the Ruhr was under threat. In these first steps towards unity in Europe, Stalin's rapacity, the Communist menace and American pressure all played their part in bringing the statesmen to their decisions and the public to their support, but without the spiritual factor operating through men and women of character and commitment, their work could hardly have been well based, with the organism that was its outcome so well adapted for further evolution.

1.David J.Heilbron Price: *Schuman, Acheson and supranationality* (paper given at the Ninth Lothian Conference, 17/12/94),10. The quotations given in the following note are from Robert Rochefort:*Robert Schuman (Paris 1968)*. Schuman (1886-1963), was born in Luxembourg, where his parents migrated from Lorraine after its cession to Germany in 1871, after the war in which his father had fought on the side of France. His higher education was at German universities, including Strasbourg (then German) where he shared the patriotism of those desiring the return of their country to France. He thought of taking holy orders, but a friend persuaded him to remain a layman 'because you will succeed better at doing good, which is your unique preoccupation...The saints of tomorrow will be the saints in jackets.' Schuman accepted the challenge, though he never thought of himself as a saint, only as 'a very imperfect instrument of a Providence which makes use of us in accomplishing great designs which go far beyond ourselves.' He represented Metz in the

French Parliament after Alsace-Lorraine was returned to France in 1918. On the defeat of France in 1940 he was imprisoned by the Gestapo and pressurized to become Gauleiter of Alsace-Lorraine, which he refused on the grounds that it would be 'rather difficult for a French MP.' He was deported to Germany but escaped, and was on the run until the liberation of France when he was re-elected MP. He was Minister of Finance 1946-7 and Prime Minister 1947-8 (when the Communists were making a bid to take over the country), then Foreign Minister until 1953.

2.Price,op.cit.,5.

3.Robert Schuman: *Pour l'Europe* (Paris 1963),66.

4.Frank Buchman: *Refaire le monde* (Paris 1950),1; translated in Frank Buchman: *Remaking the World*,347.

5.Centre de Recherches Européennes , Lausanne, printed in part in Jean-Pierre Gouzy: *Les Pionniers de l'Europe Communautaire* (published by the same institution, 1968),10. See also R.C. Mowat: *Creating the European Community* (London 1973),347.

6.François Duchène: *Jean Monnet* (New York 1994),348.

7.Ibid.,390.

8.Ibid.,88.

9.'The Tablet',3/12/94: review of Basil Hume: 'Remaking Europe: the Gospel in a divided continent' (London 1994).

10.The Keswick Convention was initiated by R.P.Smith in 1875 for annual evangelical conferences.

11.A.J.Russell: *For Sinners Only* (London 1932),58.

12.Ibid.,59.

13.Garth Lean: *Frank Buchman: a life* (London 1985), 238.

14.H.W.'Bunny' Austin: *Frank Buchman as I knew him* (London 1975), 79.

15.Ibid.,98.

CHAPTER 5

CONFERENCE WITH A NEW DIMENSION

A work of reconciliation had been started in the French zone of occupied Germany by a group of enlightened officials. In addition to cultural developments which brought French and Germans together, non-governmental bodies were encouraged to set up associations for youth and hold summer sessions which could be attended by officially sponsored parties of young French people starting with a thousand in 1946, rising to 5,000 in 1949. The fruits were long-term rather than immediate, when those involved came into responsible positions in trade unions, politics and education. On another level, surviving members of the Confessing Church, which had stood out against Hitler, expressed the need for forgiveness in the Declaration of Guilt issued in November 1945 by the Council of the newly formed German Evangelical Church.

But these actions were the work of an elite. The mass of French people were still gripped by hatred of the Germans for the humiliations and harsh treatment — sometimes torture and terrorism — which they had suffered under the occupation. Trade unionists would not attend international conferences at which Germans (though anti-Nazis) were present, and such boycotts occurred on other occasions. A change of attitude had to take place in wider circles if a policy of partnership based on reconciliation could be initiated. Schuman, as Foreign Minister during four and a half crucial years from July 1948, knew he had to wait until enough of the public were ready for such a move.

It was in this context that Moral Re-Armament made a special contribution, particularly through the Assemblies at Caux. The background was a continent half destroyed — bridges blown, roads ruined, railways and factories wrecked, some cities almost obliterated. There was shortage of food, of everything. All Europe except for the west was under military occupation. Hatred had accumulated, with the stench of the death-camps and massacres, the bereavements and the ruins, and the ruthlessness and brutality of the occupying armies. How to salvage the values of civilisation? How to bring some order out of this chaos?

One miracle was a country in the middle of Europe which had been preserved from war — Switzerland, and in the mountains above the Lake of Geneva — Caux. Caux provided the training-ground, conference centre and launching-point for an enterprise which enabled the creative work of the statesmen to be achieved.

The Caux-Palace Hotel, two thousand feet above Montreux, had been scheduled for demolition and was on the point of being sold for its fittings and building material. Built at the turn of the century on a lavish scale for guests such as Maharajahs and their retinues, it suffered a severe set-back when the 'belle époque' ended in 1914, and never fully recovered between the wars. During the second World War it housed refugees and internees, who camped in its halls and reception rooms as well as occupying bedrooms and bathrooms, with resulting dilapidations and damage. But the soundness of its structure and its superb situation made it a potential centre of the utmost worth. A group of Swiss, encouraged by Buchman, who knew the place from his early travels, decided at considerable sacrifice to buy it. They were supported in this decision by a handful of French and Germans who managed — despite the postwar limitations on travel — to attend a conference with them at Interlaken at Easter 1946. By donating capital, cashing life-insurances and selling homes the purchase price was raised, and in a few weeks the labour of volunteers and donations of furniture enabled the Assembly to open in July.

The difficulties of arranging anything like a representative German attendance at this time seemed almost insuperable. Practically no Germans were allowed to travel abroad, and the very few who managed to do so had to obtain special permission from the governments of the occupying powers and their zone commanders in Germany. In the event some 17 Germans received exit permits in 1946, among them the widows of two of the resistance leaders, von Trott and von Häften. But next year it was possible to bring 150, rising to over 1,300 in 1949. That this

39

became possible was largely due to the American dimension of the work. Kenaston Twitchell had become one of Buchman's fellow-workers while a student at Princeton in the twenties, subsequently spending several years at Oxford. His father-in-law, H. Alexander Smith, the Senator for New Jersey, arranged for him to have an interview with General George Marshall who was then Secretary of State for Foreign Affairs. This interview paved the way for another, with Robert Patterson, the Secretary of War, who promised to help remove all bottlenecks in arranging for German representation at Caux.

Visas for a visit by Twitchell and his wife to Germany were now forthcoming, and this took place shortly afterwards. The Twitchells were accompanied by two others who had been working closely with Buchman, John Roots, a journalist formerly of Harvard University, and Eugene von Teuber, an American citizen of Austrian-Czech origin. En route in London Twitchell had an interview with Lord Pakenham, the Minister in charge of the British zone of Germany, who gave his blessing to the enterprise. 'Along with food,' he said, 'the kind of work you are doing is the only thing which will do any good in Germany now.'[1] He at once took steps to ensure that visas would be available for German visitors to Caux, and a list of 55 people began to be screened. He also telephoned to General Sir Brian Robertson, Commander of the British zone, to give Twitchell and his party every facility.

An equally warm response came from General Lucius Clay, in charge of the American zone, who arranged for Twitchell and his friends to meet the political leaders of the Länder (states) of the zone at a conference in Stuttgart some days later. He gave these men no hint as to what was in store for them. The invitation to Caux as the guests of the Americans which was given to them personally, including bringing wives and families, was completely unexpected. 'Their bewilderment gradually brightened into surprise and appreciation,' wrote Twitchell. 'Most of them had not been out of Germany since 1933. Some had been in prison. The thought of their wives and children visiting a free country, with good food and friends, had been beyond their dreams. Yet from the start these men understood that they were not coming for a vacation. They began to realise the possibilities of a genuine re-creation not only for themselves and families, but also for Germany and Europe.'[2]

For several years most Germans had been living among the dreary ruins of their cities, in what was left of wrecked and leaky buildings. In the British zone especially the meagre ration standards were seldom met, and many were continually hungry – as well as cold, since fuel remained scarce. Twitchell noted that the Minister of Labour in North-Rhine Westphalia (including the Ruhr area) had to make do with 'two narrow slices of stale bread for breakfast, a few potatoes and some decaying cabbage for lunch.'

The transition from this situation to Switzerland, its cities intact, its villages neat and well painted, above all to the warmhearted welcome, the good food and the new style of life at Caux, made an indelible impression. One of the party, Peter Petersen (later a Member of Parliament in the Federal Republic), who had been indoctrinated in Nazism from the age of 12 at one of the special schools for training leaders, had been discharged from the army cynical and bitter after war service. He – no doubt like many other Germans – arrived at Caux with mixed feelings. 'I fully expected to hear people say 'what are these criminals doing here?" he relates. 'I was ready with counter-accusations to whatever we were accused of. Instead we were made welcome. A French chorus sang in German a song expressing Germany's true destiny. Every door was open to us. We were completely disarmed.'[3]

As the Berlin daily 'Tagespiegel' said: 'In one point especially were the German guests agreed, that nowhere in the world at the present time would Germans find such a welcome awaiting them as at Caux.'

Smaller but still substantial numbers of representative French citizens also came during this and subsequent years, as well as many hundreds from the rest of Europe and overseas. The impact of the meetings was constantly heightened by participants such as miners of the Ruhr, who found new life and a more satisfying ideology than Marxism, despite ferocious Communist opposition. Directors and managers followed suit, with harmony and co-operation becoming the norm in the recently established works councils.

Something of the spirit of Caux during these immediate postwar years is captured in a description by a participant.

'Mountain House and the smaller hotels around it are packed to bursting with throngs of people from almost every nation who have come to attend the World Assembly for Moral Re-Armament. You have to live with a kind of sixth sense in order to find the people whom you want to meet from among the 1,300 who are to be found in the meeting hall or dining rooms, or walking on the famous promenade from which one is tempted to throw pebbles down on Montreux and the Chateau de Chillon immediately below.

'This past weekend planes flew in to Geneva airport bringing delegations from America (including several Senators and Congressmen), from Britain, Scandinavia, Holland, Germany. An industrial delegation 70 strong (among them the directors of important firms as well as trade union leaders) arrived by train from France.

'Perhaps it is the distinguished character of the large German delegation which impresses one as much as anything. It is made up of representatives from all zones (except the Russian – but including Berlin), and all have come with the blessing of the Allied Military Governors concerned. Many people have made this possible. One of the most eminent men in Switzerland was so interested in what MRA could give to Germany that he personally financed the coming of a hundred of the delegation ...

'No wonder that Senator Harry P. Cain from the State of Washington, U.S.A., said that what he had seen at Caux had resolved the doubts which he had felt about appropriating so many billions of dollars for aid to Europe. 'I can say with conviction,' he told the Assembly, 'that these material things we give are going to give us a run for our money because behind them, and more important, the spirit first of Europe and then of the world is being rejuvenated and revitalised.'

'Caux is a worthy setting for great occasions such as the arrival of the President of the Swiss Confederation, greeted by cheers followed by silence as in perfect harmony the National Hymn of Switzerland was sung by a choir standing on the hillside. Another memorable event was the speech of Max Huber, during the war years President of the International Red Cross and formerly Supreme Judge of the International Tribunal at The Hague.

'Much of his thought, as of that of the President of the Swiss Federal Assembly who spoke later, was for Germany, and how Switzerland could make positive her traditional neutrality by helping to integrate the nation in the new Europe of tomorrow. Germany has been well in the picture here, but by no means exclusively.

'The French delegation spoke soon after the German, and one noticed how the qualities of these two nations complemented each other. There was the clearness, precision and discipline of the French mind, together with much typical French humour. There was a feeling too of comradeship and solidarity which gave fresh hope for their troubled country.'[4]

Changes of heart and mind were what Caux was all about. One of the most remarkable was that of a retired British admiral, 'Bill' Phillips, and its repercussions on several German generals who were present.[5] But for the participants as a whole the resolution of the age-old conflicts between French, Germans and British was not the main objective: the immediate postwar conferences were industrial (a carry-over from the work in America) with the aim of forging new relationships between management and labour, which meant an approach as it were on

43

the blind side to people who had been in conflict. It was a classic instance of Jean Monnet's prescription: change the context in which the problems are considered, find 'what is common in the interest of the people concerned ... direct their minds to the point where their interests converge ... put them in front of the same problem, [then] they are no longer the same people.'[6] The 'problem', which took the place of more divisive ones, came to be that of initiating partnership, eventually by way of setting up the Community of Coal and Steel.

At Caux the meetings, the meals, the teamwork with others of various nations, occupations and background made their impact. So also did the plays. One of these depicted Fredrik Ramm, the Norwegian journalist whose change had led, before the war, to his about-turn from exacerbating the Greenland fisheries dispute between Norway and Denmark to initiating conciliation between the two countries with a public apology on the radio for his previously divisive attitude – and led on to his courageous leadership in the resistance and his imprisonment by the Gestapo and consequent death. Seeing this play Reinhold Maier, the Minister-President of Württemburg-Baden, describes how he was overcome by shame at the thought of Germany's misdeeds – slinking from the hall without looking up, he threw himself on his bed completely knocked out. 'It was a presentation without hatred and complaint, and therefore could hardly have been of more powerful effect.'[7]

Another play which had a great effect was 'The Forgotten Factor' which had originated as one of the new 'weapons' envisioned by Buchman in 1940 for bringing about teamwork in American industry – a play which at Caux was equally appropriate since dealing with industrial strife was a principal aim of the assemblies. It dealt with a violent industrial confrontation and its resolution through the change in the boss's son and its effect on his father and the labour leader. As Edward Luttwak notes, 'all along, MRA's *primary emphasis* was on labor-management relations and interclass, rather than international, reconciliation.' But, he says, 'the exceptional MRA emphasis on exponents of the coal and steel industries ... turned out to be a classic case of serendipity (favorably interlinked chance, luck, providence), though it actually reflected quite a different conflict-resolution purpose ... When Schuman set out to apply Monnet's concept (informally known as the Schuman Plan), it was certainly a crucial advantage for the politicians and bureaucrats on both sides that many leading French and German coal and steel industrialists and trade union leaders had already developed warm personal relationships at Caux. If MRA had done nothing else, its ancillary role in the creation of the ECSC [European Coal and Steel Community] would alone give it importance in the history of Europe.'[8]

'The Forgotten Factor' had been sponsored for its Washington premiere in 1944 by Harry Truman, the Senator for Missouri who was shortly to take over the presidency of the USA on Franklin Roosevelt's death. Another strong supporter was Senator Arthur Vandenberg, leader of the Republicans and Chairman of the Senate Foreign Relations Committee, a war-time convert from isolationism who initiated the bi-partisan approach enabling America to take on its new world-wide responsibilities and successfully launch the Marshall Plan. Six and a half thousand people saw this and other MRA plays in Washington DC in the winter of 1947-8, many of them from government and trade union circles.

For the Germans this was a particularly crucial moment. Against the background of ruins and privation in their country the new constitution which became that of the Federal Republic was being worked out, at the same time as the new political and economic structures on a regional basis were taking shape in the Länder.

The visit to Caux of the future Chancellor, Konrad Adenauer, in 1947 was brief, but the calibre of the German delegation in that year can be gauged from those who produced the booklet 'Es muss alles anders werden' (everything has to change) – a catchphrase of the day which was the title of one of the songs in the repertoire of the Caux chorus. Among them, besides Reinhold Maier, were two former Prime Ministers of Länder, the President of the Bavarian Parliament, the Secretaries of both the Christian Democratic and Social Democratic Parties of Berlin, and many other representatives of government and the press. Radio broadcasts and press articles about this booklet and the experiences of Germans at Caux evoked many thousand letters to the radio stations and newspapers.

Next year Adenauer came with some 500 Germans. Following a performance of 'The Forgotten Factor', he said 'I consider it a notable deed that in a time when evil so openly rules in the world, people have courage to stand for good, for God, and that each one begins with himself. I believe and it is my deepest wish, as it is of all those who have come here from Germany, that the ideas of Caux will richly bring their fruits a thousandfold. This battle is in reality a life-and-death struggle, a battle between good and evil.'[9]

A particular impact on the Germans was made by Mme. Irène Laure, the former resistance leader and Socialist M.P. for Marseilles. Disillusioned after efforts in the inter-war years to build bridges between French and Germans, her hatred of the Germans became intense during the occupation, especially when her son was tortured by the Gestapo to make her reveal secrets of the resistance (which she refused to do), and when she witnessed the opening of a mass grave of the Nazis' victims. She came to Caux suspecting it to be a capitalist trap – her suspicion turned to repulsion when she found there were Germans present. She was on the point of packing her bag to leave when a talk with Buchman left her with the uncomfortable thought, 'can you build the new Europe without the Germans?' She decided to stay on and investigate further, during three days and nights of agonised pondering.

'The moment came,' she said later, 'when I had to admit that

46

hatred, however justified, will always lead to more bitterness, to more wars. Somebody had to make the first move towards breaking the vicious circle. I needed a miracle to uproot hate from my heart. I hardly believed in God but He performed that miracle. I publicly apologised to the Germans, not for my Resistance fight, but for my hatred. I had willed the total destruction of their country. In doing this I experienced such a complete liberation that it felt like 100 kilos lifted off my stomach.'[10]

It was a telling point that Mme. Laure decided not to say she forgave the Germans, but asked that they should forgive her. Peter Petersen was present, sitting ill at ease in the back of the hall at the plenary when she rose to speak. He knew of Mme. Laure's wish to leave when she had heard that Germans were present. He had decided with some of his compatriots that if she expressed her hatred they would reply with stories of the French occupation of the Black Forest. Now however her speech 'was only three sentences long — but these three sentences marked a turning point in our lives, as individuals and as Germans. She said 'I hated Germany so much that I would have liked to see it erased from the map of Europe. But I have seen here that my hatred is wrong. I would like to ask all the Germans present to forgive me.''[11]

The effect on the Germans was electric. Petersen himself could not sleep for several nights — his 'whole past was in revolt at the courage of this woman.' The full horror of the things their country had done came over the Germans. They decided to apologise personally to Mme. Laure, and publicly admit their shame at what their country had done to others, while undertaking to work in the spirit which she had shown, to rebuild Europe on new foundations.[12]

Soon afterwards Irène Laure was invited to Germany. She made several visits there, speaking to many thousands of people in the western zones and in Berlin, addressing the Länder parliaments and meeting most of the men and women who were coming forward into public life. Others from France went with her, including two men who had lost most of their family, the one fifteen and the other twenty-two, in the gas-chambers of Hitler's death camps. Such personal decisions, costly and difficult as they were, played their part in preparing the ground for the statesmen to carry through on another level the work of reconciliation, and open a new way towards the future of Western Europe. At this time tension was high since the Russians were attempting to offset the almost miraculous effects of the currency reform of June 1948 by sealing off their zone and blockading those of the Western Allies in Berlin, who undertook the colossal operation of the airlift for provisioning their beleaguered zones.

Reinforcement of the proceedings at Caux and their outreach into Germany and France came once again from America. Eighty-two Senators and Congressmen were the sponsors of an assembly in California in June 1948 to which came delegations from all over the world, including some of the Germans who had recently been at Caux. Among them were Dr. Gustav Heinemann, who was Mayor of Essen and later President of the Federal Republic, and both the President and leader of the opposition in the Bavarian Parliament. The American authorities recognised that what MRA had to give was essential for the recovery programme which they had initiated for Europe. Paul Hoffman, the Administrator of the Marshall Plan, said in a message to the Assembly 'You are the ideological counterpart of the Marshall Plan'. He hosted a lunch for the German delegates at Washington on their return journey, attended by Marshall himself, who spoke of the need for spiritual regeneration as the complement of the material foundation which the aid programme was providing.[13]

Meanwhile moves were made to enable the plays, which were having such an impact at Caux, to reach wider audiences in Germany and France. Adenauer joined with Karl Arnold, Minister-President of North-Rhine Westphalia, and other Minister-Presidents, to invite the plays to Germany. Arnold, a strong supporter of Buchman and his work, was another of the Christian leaders who had been persecuted and suppressed by the totalitarian regimes and who had come forward after their defeat. A man of

48

profound Catholic faith, Arnold had made his name between the wars as a leader of the Christian trade unions, and as the chief spokesman of the Centre Party in Düsseldorf, where — after surviving harassment and want during the Nazi era — he became Lord Mayor in 1946. His main themes in his speeches during this period were the ending of hate and the acceptance of a European patriotism in place of self-centred national egoism. He linked these aims with proposals for the internationalisation of the Ruhr (which was within his Land) by way of an association including Belgium, Luxembourg and the Saar, into which France would bring the ore-bearing region of Lorraine.[14]

The invitations for the plays opened the way for the largest civilian body, 260 strong, to enter Germany since the war. The Western authorities gave every facility, and in the autumn of 1948 the cavalcade left Switzerland to bring 'The Good Road' to the cities of Germany which, though ruined, had in many cases theatres or halls which had survived or had just been rebuilt — as at Munich, where Minister-President Ehard spoke from his box to welcome the play. Capacity audiences in five of the main cities comprised a cross-section of all walks of life.

1.Lean, op.cit.,350.

2.Kenaston Twitchell: *Regeneration in the Ruhr* (Princeton 1981), 22.

3.Lean,350.

4.R.C.Mowat: 'The Caux spirit' (New World News Agency, 23/9/48).

5.Michael Henderson: *The Forgiveness Factor* (Grosvenor Books, USA and London),28.

6.Jean Monnet: *Memoirs* (tr.Mayne, London 1978),248.

7.Reinhold Maier: *Ein Grundstein wird gelegt 1945-7* (Tübingen 1964), 383.

8.Edward Luttwak in Douglas Johnston and Cynthia Sampson: *Religion, the Missing Dimension of Statecraft* (O.U.P.New York 1994), 51-2. Dr.Luttwak is director of the Geoeconomics Project at the Center for Strategic and International Studies and former holder of the Center's Chair in Strategy. He is also a member of the Religion and Conflict Resolution Project steering group. Among his publicatons are *The Moral Nation: Humanitarianism and U.S.Foreign Policy Today* (South Bend,Ind.: University of Notre Dame Press,1989), and *The Endangered American Dream* (New York 1993).

9.Caux transcripts, extracts of speeches by German leaders at Caux, September 1948, in David J.H.Price: *The Moral Re-Armament movement and postwar European reconstruction* (unpublished thesis, London University 1979).

10.Henderson, 27.

11.R.C.Mowat: *Decline and Renewal: Europe Ancient and Modern* (New Cherwell Press, Oxford 1991), 197.

12.Idem.

13.Lean, op.cit.,355.

14.Speech of 1 August 1949, quoted in Rainer Barzel: *Karl Arnold* (Bonn 1960), 31-2.

CHAPTER 6

FROM CONFLICT TO PARTNERSHIP

In the Ruhr 1,500 from management of the mining industry requested a special performance of 'The Good Road', while Karl Arnold and other leaders invited 'The Forgotten Factor'. The cast and 50 others stayed on after the show there, based at Essen. The news of changed lives resulting from the plays was an impressive input to the Caux meetings, along with the appearance in person of many of those concerned.

The Communists in the Ruhr were in a strong position, encouraged and financed by their colleagues in the Soviet-controlled zones of East Germany. It appeared that Communist policy was to make the Ruhr in effect a Soviet enclave, an aim which, if it had been realised, might have brought grave difficulties for the Western allies in internationalising the Ruhr Authority, which turned out to be a step towards the Schuman Plan. Penetration and control by the Communists was exerted largely through the works councils, which the Allied Control Council had set up in the factories and mines, and which played a much bigger part than the trade unions in representing the workers' interests.

Leif Hovelsen was a Norwegian who met MRA through a university professor in the Grini concentration camp to which they had both been confined by the Gestapo on account of their resistance activities. On being liberated at the war's end, a strong conviction impelled him to forgive personally the man, now himself a prisoner, who had been most responsible for his sufferings at the hands of the Gestapo. He began to understand the need for reconciliation with the Germans, and cut short his university studies – a costly decision – to devote himself to this work. After a visit to Caux he joined a group at Düsseldorf, a centre of the coal-mining area with half a million miners.

'The breakdown of Nazism had led to unbelievable misery both material and spiritual. A large part of the industries was destroyed. Hundreds of thousands of homes were in ruins. Confusion, emptiness and despair reigned.'[1] But 'by reason of the results 'The Good Road' and 'The Forgotten Factor' had in the Ruhr, we soon got to know the leading men and women in the industrial, political and cultural life. The Germans took us into their homes. They shared their food rations with us, though they got very little. We slept in rooms where holes in windows were stuffed with newspaper or rags.'[2]

The Communists swiftly organised their opposition to MRA. When a performance of 'The Forgotten Factor' in Moers was announced in January 1949, a meeting was arranged by the chairman of the works council of Rheinpreussen Pit No. 4, Max Bladeck, a Communist Party member for 25 years and its representative for Moers in the party organisation for the Land. A man with a keen mind, he was one of the party's leading strategists in the area. His aim was to defeat MRA before ever it got moving in the locality.

This meeting in the Heier Tavern was in the nature of a public debate. Bladeck and five of his friends 'opened fire one after another ... The 'blitz' went on for more than an hour'. Then the MRA speakers had their turn – workers from the Clyde and the East End of London, together with a Canadian employer, Bernard Hallward, who spoke of his own change so sincerely and with so many humorous touches that he carried his audience with him. 'What has created injustices in the Western world' was his theme, 'is the selfishness and moral compromise in men like me ... The hard-boiled materialism of the right is reflected in the bitter materialism of the left.' After four hours of discussion Bladeck and his friends asked for another meeting, and they also came to see the play.[3]

For all the outward strength of Communism in the Ruhr, doubts had entered the minds of the party workers owing to the harshness of Soviet rule in the east zone and the satellite countries. Through this chink in what they could not help perceiving as the difference between Marxist theory and its actual practice the message of MRA was able to penetrate. But the challenge to which they responded was not couched in evangelical language. It was the claim that human nature – including their own – could be changed through the application of absolute moral standards. The conclusion which some of them reached, often after months of investigation, discussion and experimentation, betokened a deeper revolution than Communism. As one of the Moers miners, Paul Kurowski, put it, 'whoever refuses to live by the principles of absolute honesty, purity, unselfishness and love is a traitor to his class and country'.[4]

Kurowski and others went to the Caux conference in the summer of 1949 to pursue their investigations. At this, officials of the Communist Party in the Ruhr became alarmed, especially when one of their most promising younger members, Willi Benedens – who, on account of his Marxist convictions, had been sent to a penal battalion during the war and had lost both his legs – failed to bring them back but became a changed man himself.

'When MRA came to Moers,' he said later, 'I attacked it as violently as I could.' But eventually he decided to find out what lay behind it and went to Caux. 'In Caux I found the thing I had been fighting for through years – a classless society. I experienced a personal change. Previously I had thought only of politics and the party and not of my wife and children. I often quarrelled with my wife ... Was I one hundred per cent socialist? I was working for peace and understanding between nations but there was war in my own home and strife between me and my neighbours.'[5]

This was typical of the convictions which came to such men. Frequently, on the personal level, it was to remake a relationship with their wives, and to put things right in their homes. Fritz Heske was one of the veterans in the fight for Communism in the Essen area, having been thrown into prison for two years by the Nazis for organising resistance against them. When the regime collapsed he started to rebuild the party in his area, with a cell of a hundred men at the pit where he was chairman of the works council.

By the time his interest in MRA was aroused a directive had come from party headquarters that Communists were not to attend its meetings, and he was specifically forbidden to go to one at Königswinter where the chairmen of the works councils had been invited by the management – of whom some had also reached the point of making decisions that were revolutionising their life-style and relations with the work-force. He had nonetheless gone, for, as he said, 'am I not the representative of the workers and should I not form my own opinion in order to be able to answer the questions the workers are always putting to me about MRA?' For this he was expelled from the party, from which his son, who till then had been a keen party worker, thereupon resigned.

This opposition served only to strengthen Heske's new convictions. But the home was the decisive area for his change to come to fruition. For the first time father and son were completely open and honest with each other. And the impact on Frau Heske was equally great.

The opposition from the Communist apparatus became increasingly bitter. In spite of the party's veto on the visit, Bladeck and Kurowski went to Caux a second time. The new imperatives for them were the priority of God's guidance (in terms of 'conscience') and the fight against evil. When summoned by the party for their contravention of discipline, the thought of one of them was 'I will let my conscience guide me and do what it says. It will determine my life.' Another thought was 'a revolutionary's life is a battle. It is also a battle against the evil within oneself.'[6] They were duly expelled. Kurowski was howled down at his last meeting when he tried to speak, and was driven from the room.

Meanwhile the rank and file of the workers rallied behind those who had committed themselves to MRA. At the ensuing elections to the works councils those who held positions as chairmen or members were all re-elected with increased majorities, despite ferocious Communist attempts to unseat them. By 1950 Communist membership of the councils had dropped from 72% to 25%.

'Exactly how much the improved industrial relations and decline of Communist influence in the Ruhr should be attributed to Moral Re-Armament is impossible to assess accurately,' writes Garth Lean.[7] 'Other obvious influences were the improving material position of the workers in the wake of both the Marshall Plan and the currency reform, the introduction of new technology, the news of conditions in the East brought back by prisoners of war and millions of refugees, and the progress of other political parties as they rebuilt their party machines.'

Chancellor Adenauer, however, had no doubts about what he called 'the great success which the team of Moral Re-Armament had achieved in the Ruhr', in a message which he sent to a meeting of over 2,000 at the mining town of Gelsenkirchen in May 1950. 'Moral Re-Armament has become a household word in postwar Germany,' he went on. 'Wide circles of men in politics, in industry, and in the trade unions have come in contact with the ideas of Moral Re-Armament. In addition, countless leading politicians, leaders in the trade union movement, in industry and in business have been invited to take part in the yearly conferences in Caux. They are grateful that Caux has given them the opportunity of discussing Germany's burning problems on a world basis and in an atmosphere of cordial co-operation, with representatives from every country where individual freedom is still preserved. I believe that in view of the offensive of totalitarian ideas in the East, the Federal Republic, and within it the Ruhr, is the given platform for a demonstration of the idea of Moral Re-Armament.'[8]

The Hans Sachs House at Gelsenkirchen, holding far more than its supposed 2,000 capacity, was the venue for something like a day of the Caux conference. 'Miners, steelworkers, leaders of industry and politics, people from all parts of the Ruhr and from all over Germany were there. A group of men and women from the Russian-occupied zone had risked coming across the border and making the long journey in order to attend. Among the many

55

representatives from some twenty-four other nations was the widow of Burma's first Prime Minister, Aung San; the chairman of the million strong Japanese railways workers, Etsu Kato; Irène Laure; and the elderly Senator Theodore Green, one of Roosevelt's close colleagues.'[9]

Buchman was staying for the occasion at the home of Hans Dütting, the Director of the Gelsenkirchen Coal-Mining Company. Dütting had gone to Caux in 1949 hoping for a holiday and some mountain climbing. But the visit made him alter completely his business methods. 'We began quite spontaneously to give our workers' representatives more information. The result was an extraordinary growth in trust between work-force and management. Every month I have a special meeting with all chairmen of works councils, some twenty-five in all. Absolute honesty prevails. Each side knows that no one in that gathering is telling an untruth. Perhaps I gave myself the strongest push towards a change in our mutual attitudes when I spoke openly about a wrong decision I had made, which I then put straight with the help of the works councillors.'[10]Bladeck and his fellow-workers had been amazed to hear similar words from Heinrich Kost, the head of the German Coal Board and Chairman of Directors of the mining company centred in Moers.

This changed approach of directors and managers in the Ruhr supplies a clue as to how the proceedings for working out the details in applying the Schuman Plan went through so speedily, enabling them to be set forth in the treaty of 'the Six' which was signed within a year — a record for dealing with such vast and complex issues as were involved.

The way forward was determined as much by economic considerations as political. As Monnet had foreseen in his wartime memorandum (1943),[11] the creation of a European 'entity' without frontier-posts and tariff barriers would be necessary to ensure 'the prosperity which modern conditions make possible,' for which purpose the countries of Europe were 'too cramped' in their existing situation. In fact it was within the national framework that Monnet found he had to begin his postwar work, persuading de Gaulle of the necessity of a national plan for the modernisation and equipment of France, for which he was given the responsibility. He was backed in this by André Philip, the Minister of Finance and National Economy.

Philip was another of those committed Christians who architected the new Europe. He had made his mark before the war as an economist and university professor who had become a socialist and gone into politics because of his Christian convictions. He was a Protestant, descended from Camisard ancestors who had fought to maintain their faith in the Cevennes against the dragonnades of Louis XIV. He believed in the kind of socialism propounded by the Belgian reformer, Henri de Man − a workers' movement 'in the name of all those spiritual values − the ideal of equality, the sentiment of human dignity, the desire for justice and caring − which Christianity has brought to the world'.[12]

The Soviet blockade of Berlin (June 1948-May 1949) − an attempt to hamper the Western allies in their currency reform and other plans, or even to exclude them altogether − had further alerted them to the Communist danger. A switch in policy followed. Western Germany, under their control, had to be built up as an ally against Communism. The currency reform went ahead, the prelude to the 'economic miracle' which enabled the Federal Republic to emerge from the ruins as a productive state beginning to resume the position held by pre-war Germany as the hub of Europe's economy.

America was giving the lead, with a dynamic group at the State Department under Dean Acheson, backed by President Truman and bi-partisan Senators. Dismantling of German industry (the original Western punitive policy) was ended, and its reconstruction was facilitated by the vast programme of aid initiated by General Marshall when Secretary of State in 1947, which equally benefited the economies of Britain, France and other West European states. By 1949 over-production in certain lines, notably steel-making, was replacing shortages.

As André Philip pointed out, this was a problem which could not be solved within the confines of the nation-state. He was the French representative on the U.N. Economic Commission for Europe, and strongly backed the report of his colleague Rollman, head of the ECE's Steel Division: radical change was needed to eliminate the inefficiency and costliness of the existing system, where each country not merely worked out its own plans for production without any reference to its neighbours, but entered into a series of bilateral agreements while fiercely protecting its own domain by systems of import and export quotas, licences and tariffs – with the result that the cost of primary products was being kept at levels well above world prices. Discussion of these problems, suggested the report, and agreements aimed at solving them 'should take place within the framework of Europe as a whole.'[13] A supra-national 'public authority for steel' should be set up as the agency for harmonising production and investment on a European basis.

Similar questions arose in connection with the production and distribution of coal. This concerned particularly the area of the Ruhr, which contained not only the Federal Republic's coal-mines, but which was also the home of Krupps and other armaments factories. At the war's end French policy had been to detach the Ruhr from Germany and bring it directly under their control. Now with the setting up of the Federal Republic this was impracticable, while the inclusion of France in the International Authority for the Ruhr did not go far enough, since Anglo-American policy was to confine it to allocating the coal and steel produced in the Ruhr, but with no control over the industry itself. It was clear that the Federal Republic, constituted in May 1949, would soon demand the abandonment of all controls by the former occupying powers.

André Philip had already proposed that the Ruhr Authority, with enlarged powers for production, sales and pricing, should be extended to the whole of northern Europe: it should become 'a public inter-European service for coal and steel, the first concrete experiment in uniting Europe.'[14] When Ernest Bevin, Britain's Foreign Secretary, proposed including the Federal Republic in the Ruhr Authority, there seemed a possibility that it might undertake this role.

Schuman agreed that rebuilding the German economy was a necessary part of restoring Europe, but the question was how to enable Germany to make her contribution to recovery and yet prevent her from regaining her strength to the point where she could once again be capable of posing a military threat to her neighbours. 'A new framework is needed,' he said in the French Assembly (Parliament). 'Europe will be the building in which we will make every effort to install peace once and for all ... The future Germany will have to be inserted into this building, first on the economic level, then on the political. The Ruhr ought to be a first, a precious, an indispensable contribution to the European association which is emerging.'[15]

While the United States, through Acheson, was pressing Schuman to determine France's policy in regard to integrating the Federal Republic in Western Europe, he had to proceed warily. Any onesided concessions to Germany would tilt the balance of forces at home against him. 'We were in an impasse,' he said later. 'In order to advance we had to open a breach ... We felt the need of some psychological leap forward.'[16]

This leap into the future was provided by Monnet. With his Modernisation Plan brains-trust he had been working on drafts for what became known as the Schuman Plan, which Schuman presented to his colleagues in Cabinet, minutes after Adenauer had endorsed it by telephone from Bonn (9 May 1950).

In taking on the role during the last twenty years of the champion of European unity, France always had peace as the essential aim to be pursued. But Europe has not been made, and we have had war. Europe will not make herself all at once ... She will make herself by concrete achievements, creating first of all a real unity. The French Government

proposes to place the totality of the Franco-German production of coal and steel under a common High Authority, in an
organisation open to the participation of the other countries of
Europe. The unity of production, which will thus be tied
together, will demonstrate that any war between France and
Germany will become not only unthinkable but materially
impossible.[17]

Within a year the Treaty of Paris was signed by France, the
Federal German Republic, Italy, the Netherlands, Belgium and
Luxembourg, incorporating the proposals of the Schuman Plan.
Partnership, instead of hereditary enmity, was established between
France and Germany, and the first European Community was
launched. In August 1952 the High Authority, chaired by Monnet,
began its operations in Luxembourg for establishing a common
market and agreed methods of investment and production for the
coal and steel industries of 'the Six'.

One of the chief negotiators commented that the Schuman
talks were 'of a cordiality unequalled in [his] experience.' The
proceedings had ended in a way strikingly unusual for any such
major diplomatic event. 'While Schuman and the Quai d'Orsay
looked on in wonder, the Belgian delegation led the others in
singing a ballad of its own composition on the Schuman Plan.
Hallstein [the German delegate], not usually one for levity, led in
a parody of the Nazi Horst Wessel hymn ... A divide had been
crossed. Much of the later resilience of European policy was
rooted in the corporate feeling developed in the Schuman conference.'[18]

For six years, at a cost of sixty million lives, wars and
massacres on a horrific scale had spun the world into a vortex of
immeasurable violence. With the war's end there was an obvious
need for a peace based on reconciliation. Wholesale destruction
and slaughter left hearts and minds as well as cities in ruin.
Moreover as the sounds of war fell silent, the stories of inflicted
sufferings of a gross and brutal kind, the harvest of the Satanic

parodies of the Christian faith, gave warning of the rise of new enmities. An extreme of evil had to be met by an extreme of good. This was the challenge facing world leaders. In Europe the historic ways of dealing with disputes gave way to new approaches and new institutions. In this revolutionary change the part played by dedicated Christians is striking.

Kant's vision was being realised. In this instance at least, the human race was being educated to abandon war, and substitute motives of caring and mutual helpfulness for methods of aggression and violence. Prophetic voices down the centuries had stressed that the alternative to destroying people and cities, along with civilisation and even the habitat, was to build unity in home, workplace, community and country. Now the vision of change on a continental scale had brought people to face decisively the challenge of personal change, and so make possible the constructive work of the statesmen. It is a vision which must not be lost.

1.Leif Hovelsen: *Out of the Evil Night* (London 1959), 60.
2.Idem.
3.Ibid.,68.
4.Ibid.,70.
5.Ibid.,71.
6.Ibid.,73.
7.Lean,362.
8.Hovelsen,95.
9.Ibid.,96.
10.Lean,369.
11.'Réalités' (Paris), Christmas 1962, François Fontaine: *L'homme qui change le monde sous nos yeux*, reprinted under the title *Jean Monnet* by the Centre de Recherches Européennes, University of Lausanne (1963),13.

12.André Philip: *Socialisme et rationalisation,* in *Henri de Man et la crise doctrinale du socialisme* (Paris 1928), 53. See also *André Philip par lui-même* (Paris 1971).

13.Information to author from M.Tony Rollman; Rollman Report, p.72, quoted in Henri Rieben: *Des Ententes de maîtres de forges au Plan Schuman* (Lausanne 1954), 315; R.C.Mowat: *Creating the European Community* (London 1973),88.

14.Idem.

15.Journal Officiel XXI (Débats - Assemblée Nationale), 7346.

16.Robert Rochefort: *Robert Schuman* (Paris 1968), 264.

17.Schuman, op.cit.,201ff.

18.Duchène, op.cit.,219,220.

CHAPTER 7

ENDING CIVIL WAR: RHODESIA AND ZIMBABWE

As in the case of the resolution of the French/German conflict, peacemaking in Zimbabwe can be regarded as a demonstration of Christianity in action, not only among well-intentioned whites but equally among blacks: committed Christians who succeeded eventually in taking advantage of the conflict becoming 'ripe' for resolution.[1] Ron Kraybill, who wrote the relevant section in *Religion, the Missing Dimension of Statecraft*, gives ten pages each to the work for reconciliation by the Roman Catholic Church, Moral Re-Armament and the Quakers. In this work the three 'streams' from the Renaissance were again flowing together.[2]

'The three groups shared a striking similarity: all dealt with the 'entry' problem by the use of listening strategies. Individuals from both the Quakers and MRA teams repeatedly emphasized in later interviews the importance of low-key, nonjudgmental listening to the parties as a central part of their work, and both organizations spent enormous amounts of time doing it ... The groups focused on different aspects of the problem because they defined the problem itself differently, and the strategies they employed differed accordingly. But the effect of the three involvements proved to be complementary in nature. The Catholics and the Quakers recognized this and cooperated throughout the war years by keeping each other well informed about their respective activities. Contacts between MRA and the other two groups were minimal, however, and this seems a regrettable gap. Closer cooperation − if only in the sharing of information and insights about the conflict − particularly between the Quakers and MRA might have substantially enhanced the work of both organizations.'[3]

Four missions to Africa between 1972 and 1980 'formed the heart of the Quaker contribution,' with London also the scene of

63

important action. In the course of these missions the Quakers quickly etablished relationships of trust with the African leaders, Robert Mugabe, Joshua Nkomo and others. Their mode of 'entry' was their humble expression of sympathy with the various parties to the conflict 'as human beings suffering from a ghastly war and struggling to find their way out ... No other individuals or organisations maintained active communication with so broad a network of actors in the web of political influence at work in the conflict ... If expressing concern for human suffering opened doors for the Quakers, practising disciplined listening opened hearts ... [It] opened the doors for further conversation, for increasingly the parties became eager to know what the Quakers were hearing from *other* parties. The Quakers were diligent not to betray confidencies but found that their own growing knowledge of the situation soon became a resource eagerly sought by the parties ... Listening was itself a genuine contribution to change ... [They] at all times presented themselves as quiet servants of the needs of the parties. Theirs was the politics of transformative listening ... A sense of transcendent calling is more sustaining than pragmatic ambition, and the Quakers, faithful to their call, persevered in the face of long odds and major setbacks ... A U.N. diplomat commented some years later that it was widely recognized that 'the Quakers had played an important part in creating the conditions for a satisfactory settlement.''[4]

The Catholics, for the most part, says Ron Kraybill, 'defined the problem as *structural* — the political and economic structures were fundamentally unjust and needed to be overhauled. This required mobilizing opinion against existing structures via publications and lobbying efforts.'[5] The primary role of the Catholic Church was 'truth-telling', to the whites in Rhodesia and the world in general, about what was going on there. It was a change of roles, from being until 1969 a 'sanctifier of the white-dominated status quo.'[6] In that year, four years after the Smith government's Unilateral

Declaration of Independence from Britain, the government attempted to impose a complete separation of the races on all Church institutions. The consequence was a head-on clash. The Catholics, together with Protestant colleagues, openly disobeyed, the Catholics threatening to close their 'vast network of schools and hospitals. Church and state compromised in the end: the state agreed not to enforce the act, and the churches agreed to withdraw their opposition. But from this point onward the Catholic Church became a persistent and aggressive critic of the Salisbury government.'[7]

To this end the Catholics established their Commission for Justice and Peace (JPC), based at Salisbury (Harare), in liaison with the Catholic Institute for International Relations at London. Events like the counter-terrorist atrocities of the Rhodesian forces were made known 'to Whitehall and the world with a rapidity and accuracy that was acutely damaging to the image of the Rhodesian Front.'[8] They backed up these reports by visits of delegations to London and other capitals. At the same time they were even-handed, their bishops publicly deploring atrocities by the guerrillas. Eventually they took on a new role as advocates for negotiations. At short notice two bishops and a JPC member were able to have a meeting with Pope John Paul II, who immediately supported their case through Vatican diplomats in London, Washington and elsewhere. 'The Catholic Church in Rhodesia,' concludes Kraybill, 'demonstrates the potential of religious organizations to cut through the lethargy of blind patriotism to a genuinely moral basis of analysis and action[9] ... The magnitude and scope of the Catholic efforts, particularly at truth-telling, make it virtually certain that the conflict would have been prolonged and the human toll thus substantially higher had the Church not been so deeply involved.'[10]

'Moral Re-Armament is simultaneously the easiest and the hardest to assess of the three major groups in this case study,' writes Kraybill. Its most obvious contribution to the peace process was

in arranging for Ian Smith to meet his arch-opponent Robert
Mugabe soon after the end of the poll which brought Mugabe to
power. 'The Mugabe-Smith meeting without a doubt altered the
history of the nation. It is certain that white Rhodesians would
have fled the country in far greater numbers had it not been for
the conciliatory mood between Mugabe and Smith resulting from
this MRA-arranged meeting' — and for the conciliatory statements
which each of them made on the radio.[11]

Yet conciliation and settlement of disputes was secondary in
the work, for instance of Henry Macnicol, who spent ten years in
the country. 'Conflict resolution', he said, 'was not the primary
aim but the by-product of people changing to implement God's
plan [12]... You can change the system all you like but unless you
change the hearts of men, you are changing nothing.'[13]

'MRA hoped to support social change,' continues Kraybill,
'but sought to do so by way of individual change ... Their task
was to enable individuals to listen to God. This would lead to a
change of heart and to clarity about the 'right' thing to do. And if
leaders would get themselves oriented in the right direction,
society must follow.'[14]

Henry Macnicol is one of the MRA workers from Britain who had
a long period in Rhodesia/Zimbabwe. Another, Ian Robertson,
stayed on in a university post. Long visits by others, of months or
years, made it possible for MRA to contribute significantly to the
ending of the guerilla war and the eventual launching of the new
state in conditions of peace, besides arranging the last-minute
meeting of Mugabe and Smith. Hugh Elliott, who made several
lengthy visits, had a background of valuable experience as a civil
servant in Nigeria, ending a distinguished career there as Chief
Secretary of the Eastern Region.

These people, and wives, all had many years in MRA, and
shared in the same spiritual dynamic. Among newcomers to the
core group was Alec Smith, son of Prime Minister Ian Smith, who
in 1965 had made the Unilateral Declaration of Independence

(UDI). Alec's particular dynamism came from dramatic experiences which changed radically his life as a drug-taking dropout expelled from university. It was literally a call from God.

'I was driving home, high of course, when I heard a voice apparently coming from the back seat of my car. The voice said, 'Go home and read the New Testament.' I nearly jumped out of my skin.' He stopped and looked round the car – there was no one there. Eventually, at home, to his surprise he found in his drawer a Bible which he could not remember ever possessing. He began to read St. Matthew. 'I'd never really understood it before, but now it was like a wonderful new revelation. I couldn't put it down ... Then two acquaintances, one 'a really heavy hippie', unexpectedly invited him to a church service where he felt that 'the Holy Spirit had come into the building and was there with us. And then I saw Jesus Christ. He was standing in front of me ... I saw his physical presence, the light, the warmth, the outstretched arms, and I knew that he was asking me to give my life to him.'[15]

This was the beginning of a spiritual odyssey that brought Alec Smith first to a realisation of the ill-treatment and exploitation of the Africans in their own country by the whites, then to the conviction that 'what was needed was a body of Christians who were prepared under God, to work among our political leaders.' Wondering how this could be done, he 'met a most extraordinary group of people. They came from all sorts of different churches and from every walk of life. Some were students, some were civil servants. Some were university lecturers, some were housewives. They had drawn together through the work of Moral Re-Armament ... The one thing they had in common was the conviction that God, through the power of the Holy Spirit, could not only change the lives of men, but change the lives of nations.'[16]

Before long he was helping to organise an international conference (1975), which took place in the university buildings in the capital. In his speech he said 'I have come to realise that I had a personal responsibility for my country's dilemma. It was me,

Alec Smith, who was answerable because my selfish lifestyle and insensitive attitudes had finally driven those boys into the bush ... They're Rhodesians — abused, humiliated, frustrated Rhodesians ... For my part I am deeply sorry for the thoughtlessness of my past life and I have now committed myself to finding a solution for our country; to building bridges of reconciliation and to showing the rest of Africa that black and white can live together. That, under God, there is an answer.'[17]

One particularly notable response came from Arthur Kanodereka, who had been taking a leading part in encouraging young blacks to join the guerilla forces. Kanodereka was a Methodist minister, though ministering exclusively to blacks (he had been three times imprisoned and brutally tortured by the Government security forces). But, on listening to Alec Smith's apology he had a vision of what could happen. He 'saw Christ, the suffering Christ, not just for blacks, and not just for whites but for all people. A care for white people that they should find something new came into my heart and I felt a new authority from God to give his message of reconciling love to all people, regardless of the colour of their skins ... I felt my hatred fall away.'[18]

There developed between the two men a deep friendship and a working alliance which brought new hope to many people. Kanodereka began to welcome whites as well as blacks to his church, and asked Alec to join with him in giving these Sunday evening congregations a new kind of service in which the two of them 'were a sort of visual aid that black and white could not only live together, but actually work with each other and share the same ideals and goals for their society.' Kanodereka began holding weekly meetings of his congregation to meet whites and 'dialogue with them' — once as many as 800 attended. Smith and Kanodereka also made visits together in Rhodesia, South Africa and elsewhere, 'offering in classic MRA style first-person accounts of their own experiences of the power of God to bring change and reconciliation'.[19]

Meanwhile others, such as Professor Desmond Reader at the

university, were building new relationships between black and white. Reader apologised to a colleague, Gordon Chavunduka, for underestimating his abilities, which paved the way for the two of them to arrange a series of lunch and dinner parties in which responsible people from both sides of the divide were brought together - in many cases a new experience for them.[20]

These and other initiatives paved the way for the Lancaster House Conference of 1979, when the leaders and other representatives of both sides of the conflict met together under the chairmanship of the Foreign Secretary, Lord Carrington, to work out how to transfer Rhodesia, by way of an election, to an African-led government under its new name of Zimbabwe. During the 13 weeks of the conference, members of all three groups, Roman Catholics, Quakers and MRA, continued with their good work, arranging meetings and hospitality (with rest times) for delegates.

After the meeting in 1975 which brought Kanodereka and Alec Smith together, the latter joined an interracial group 'who were also concerned to bring the civil war to an end.' It came to be known as 'the Cabinet of Conscience'. 'We rarely prayed formally,' he says, 'but we did insist on a time of quiet after each discussion in which we could listen to God. It was during these periods of silence that ideas would come to us; people in government that we should approach, meetings we should hold ... '[21]

From another group of young men and civil servants came the decisive move which secured the transition to freedom and democracy in Zimbabwe without further bloodshed. It was at the end of the election week when Robert Mugabe headed the poll with a clear majority − a bitter blow to diehard whites who regarded Mugabe as the next thing to the Devil incarnate, and were planning a coup to avert his accession to power. At a meeting of this group Joram Kucherera, who had connections with Mugabe's party, insisted that Mugabe and Ian Smith had to meet. Despite scepticism on the part of his friends, he rang a cousin who was one of Mugabe's aides, and the historic meeting of Mugabe and Smith was duly arranged. Both men struck strongly a note of reconciliation in speeches which they made soon after, calling for everyone, black and white, to work together to build the new country.[22] This was one of the 'miracles' which happened 'every time we thought the thing would explode in our faces', said Lord Soames who had been appointed Governor to oversee the transition.[23]

Sadly by then Kanodereka was dead, murdered by a hit squad probably operating under those who had been planning the anti-Mugabe coup. But his work had not been in vain. Alec Smith had arranged meetings between him and his father at the Smiths' residence. 'When Dad met Arthur,' writes Alec, 'it was the first time he had ever met a black nationalist socially ... When Arthur and his wife Gladys came to tea, that was a revolution in itself ... But the two men just sat and talked. They didn't get embroiled in any great political arguments. Arthur ... just wanted to know who this Ian Smith was. There was no longer a trace of hatred in him and Dad was bowled over by his sincerity and his courage.' After the guests had gone Smith said 'Alec, I really want to thank you for bringing Arthur and Gladys here. If all black nationalists were like him, I'd have no trouble handing over the country tomorrow.' So the way was paved for the eventual meeting between Mugabe and Smith.[24] From his side Mugabe and his team 'had been working on unity as a theme of political leadership for months previously.'[25]

The Zimbabwe settlement, followed by Namibia, 'was the first to demonstrate that applied democracy is a valuable peace-making concept for ending civil war.'[26] These words, indicating a chapter of history which began with the Zimbabwe settlement and continues today, are by Allan Griffith, who had a significant part, along with the Australian Prime Minister Malcolm Fraser (to whom he was a Special Adviser on foreign policy) in the proceedings which led up to the settlement.[27]

Griffith adds:

'The diplomacy of peace-building is often protracted and demanding of domestic political resources. Governments once committed have to show patience and resourcefulness ... Mrs Thatcher found it difficult to deny her early inclination to recognise the internal settlement [which had been arranged by Ian Smith with Bishop Abel Muzorewa as the figure-head Prime Minister in 1978]. The decision of the Commonwealth Conference at Lusaka in 1979 to hold an all party constitutional conference at Lancaster House might well have foundered but for the strong solidarity of the Commonwealth and the coalition built by the Commonwealth Secretary-General and Malcolm Fraser ...

'It is clearly a world where state power administered multi-nationally provides promise for a new order. The important point is that techniques of international supervision are applicable under conditions where transparency is essential in the formula for settlement. Ancillary religious and humanitarian resources need to be identified in advance for their relevance in a given situation, and should become a more accustomed feature of diplomacy. In Zimbabwe and Namibia all parties had access to counsellors who happened to be in touch with each other. The role of the Churches and other transnational non-governmental actors as communicators and facilitators has been attested but somewhat underestimated by the official parties ...

'In bringing Zimbabwe and Namibia to independence and Cambodia to a new and hopeful political dispensation,' Griffith continues, 'democratic legitimation, as part of a system of conflict resolution, has established itself as a viable peace-making tool ... The special common feature was the use of a transitional system to displace the authority of the old state temporarily as the precondition of a cease-fire and the implementation of agreed arrangements of legitimation.

'In retrospect it can be seen that the work done during the Carter administration in cooperation with the British government and the British Foreign Secretary, Dr Owen, undertaken at the height of the Cold War, broke new frontiers of conflict resolution. Kissinger, cooperating with the British government, had provided the initial momentum, which continued collaboration between the two governments upheld in the drive for a settlement based on the principles of majority rule in Zimbabwe ... The Anglo-American proposals laid an important foundation for Lusaka to commission the Lancaster House negotiations, which in turn stimulated the search for consensus for an implementation agreement for SCR 435, which became a precedent of active significance to the Cambodia diplomacy ...

'What was to be implemented in transition relied heavily on the Governor [appointed under the Lancaster House agreements] as the transitional authority, controlling the Rhodesian armed forces. Under Lancaster House, the Patriotic Front, along with the other internal political parties, was excluded from administration. This provision was similar in effect to Security Council Resolution 435 ... The interwoven system of international supervision ensured reasonable processes of impartiality. In Zimbabwe there were times when this was secured through the efficiency of an informal system of intensive third party observation ...

'Resolution 435 of September 1978 conceded South Africa's de facto authority over the administration in Namibia. In essence, international monitoring of both transitions worked to make the incumbent administrations the servants of impartiality ... The Zimbabwe negotiation set the date of implementation, a missing factor in the plan for Namibia and a major defect. The fact, however, that the principle of an impartial transfer of power package had worked in Zimbabwe, and was still 'in principle' in being in the UN, continued to sustain the hope that implementation would not be far away ... [In fact] implementation of 435 which looked unmeaningful at the beginning of 1988 came fully into life. The transition became a shared task of the UN and the incumbent South Africa, an important variation on the successful, but essentially sui generis transition of the Zimbabwe settlement.

'The unexpected success of the Namibia settlement, drawing

72

as it did on the Zimbabwe precedent, had a profound and benefi-
cial impact on the policies of South Africa. Namibia proved that
white and black could share power in an intelligible process. The
immediate effect was to touch off a dynamic of change initiated
by the release of Nelson Mandela in February 1990, thus authenti-
cating a dialogue which ended apartheid. It is not stretching a
point too far to say that the pioneering working models in peace-
building and reconciliation in Zimbabwe and Namibia challenged
the apparently irreconcilable forces in South Africa, thereby
avoiding a catastrophic dénouement'.

In Zimbabwe the Commonwealth carried through the work of
democratic legitimation which in Namibia was undertaken by the
United Nations. The fact that the UN was in a position to do this
was another feature of the postwar Christian counter-attack. It had
been founded in 1945 in the same spirit of idealism with which
Woodrow Wilson had initiated the League of Nations after World
War I. Despite the action it had been able to take at the time of
the Korean War in 1950, it had not progressed far beyond being
a talking-shop until Dag Hammarskjöld took over as Secretary-
General in 1953.

Hammarskjöld carried into his work at the United Nations the
same Christian dedication and ideals of public service which had
been the hall-mark of his family in Sweden for several generations. He brought human rights to be one of the major concerns
of the UN, and initiated its role in peace-keeping. It was a critical
moment when the Soviet Union was trying to take over the UN
with its 'troika' proposals. 'More than any other single influence,'
says his biographer, 'his leadership transformed the UN from a
forum of prolix and often ineffectual talk into an instrument of
action by the Community of Nations for the safeguarding of peace
and the furtherance of world order.'[28]

'He was a breath of fresh air, a great man away ahead of his
time, who left, as an inspiration and an ideal, his vision of the UN
as a constitutional organisation, high above the individual nations.'

Such was the evaluation of Lord Hurd, who often met him when a young diplomat in New York.[29]

'The confidence in UN capability to deliver peace may have waned since 1989,' Allan Griffith continues. 'It is nevertheless reasonable to argue that the very successful methodology of settlement exemplified in southern Africa and Cambodia has still a large part to play in the development of the UN's future repertoire of conflict resolution ...

'The continuing practical value of the democratic legitimation formula is strengthened by a world conscious of the need to uphold the right to demand a vote where it is being denied. It remains that the Zimbabwe and Namibia settlements were the first to demonstrate that applied democracy is a valuable peace-making concept for ending civil war. There is a need for caution in ultimate expectations. A successful application of democracy anticipates but does not obviate the task of nation building which, in turn, raises the need to attend to the structural questions present in or concealed by the resolved conflict. Nevertheless the growing trend to treat democratic legitimacy as one of the most elemental tests of international obligation offers a basis for framing criteria for stable and internationally accountable government. This is an argument for giving weight to the continuing adjustment of international theory to accommodate more comfortably a greater emphasis on the UN's role sustaining democratic principles in peace-making formulas. The United Nations is structured to deliver impartiality – a central ingredient of democratic legitimation – with fairness and firmness.'

The Rhodesia/Zimbabwe settlement owed its success to the same range of factors as had brought the French/German conflict to a successful conclusion. There were the grass-roots changes of hearts and minds, brought about by small creative groups whose dynamism originated in profound and decisive spiritual experiences, such as those of Frank Buchman and Alec Smith.

At the level of statesmanship and diplomacy, similar effects

74

of the postwar Christian counter-revolution are to be observed, whether in the 'miracle' experiences of Lord Soames or in the sense of guidance transcending the merely human which characterised the wisdom of Fraser's self-effacing Adviser Allan Griffith.

1.Johnston and Sampson, op.cit.,256 (note 176). Ron Kraybill is the director of training at the Centre for Conflict Resolution (formerly Centre for Intergroup Studies) at the University of Cape Town, South Africa. He is author of *Repairing the Breach: Ministering in Community Conflict* (Scottdale, Penn.: Herald Press, 1981).
2.See above,p.30,and Chapter 10.
3.Ibid.,op.cit.,246.
4.Ibid.,236,243.
5.Ibid.,245.
6.Ibid.,212.
7.Ibid.,213.
8.Ibid.,214.
9.Ibid.,222.
10.Ibid.,246.
11.Ibid.,231.
12.Johnston and Sampson,229.
13.Henderson: op.cit.,146.
14.Idem.
15.Alec Smith: *Now I call him Brother* (Marshalls, Basingstoke 1984) 38ff.
16.Ibid.,55.
17.Ibid.,63.
18.Ibid.,64.
19.Johnston and Sampson, 226.
20.Hugh P.Elliott: *Darkness and Dawn in Zimbabwe* (Grosvenor, London 1978),19.

21. Alec Smith, 84,85.
22. Ibid.,117ff., Johnston and Sampson, 223ff., Henderson, 143ff.
23. Henderson,131.
24. Alec Smith, 84,85.
25. Johnston, 252 (note 84).
26. These and following quotations are from Allan Griffith: *Peace-Building through the Ballot Box* (to be published).
27. Griffith (b. 1922) was Adviser to successive Prime Ministers of Australia on foreign and defence policy, 1952-83.
28. H.P. Van Dusen: *Dag Hammarskjöld* (London 1967),4.
29. BBC2 TV programme, 16/11/97.

III: INTERNATIONAL RELATIONS
IN THE INFORMATION AGE

CHAPTER 8

RELIGION, THE MISSING DIMENSION
OF STATECRAFT

The title of the chapter is that of the book by Douglas Johnston and Cynthia Sampson (1994).[1] Johnston calls the section of his conclusions *Looking Ahead: Toward a New Paradigm*. The word, according to Martin Hollis and Steve Smith,[2] means 'a set of very broad assumptions whose falsity is almost unthinkable and a set of institutional practices governing the current conduct of [International Relations]' − IR, as it is known in the profession. Johnston is mainly concerned with the practices: 'the purpose of this book,' he says,' is to help fill a telling gap in the literature [about IR] and to provide insights that will enable policymakers and others [diplomats doubtless included] to comprehend and reinforce the positive contribution that religious or spiritual influences can bring to peacemaking.'[3]

Regarding the assumptions, Johnston's concern is to highlight 'the transformational possibilities that exist when the parties involved in a conflict can be appealed to on the basis of shared spiritual convictions or values. Implicit in the latter is the prospect that, under the right conditions, the parties can operate at a higher level of trust than would otherwise be possible in the realm of realpolitik.'[4] His colleague Stanton Burnett,[5] in the section *Implications for the Foreign Policy Community*, attacks the assumptions of realpolitik practitioners: 'dogmatic secularism and materialistic determinism ... a set of attitudes that, in themselves, would be enough to lead U.S. diplomacy into a state of indifference to the spiritual elements described in this study.'[6]

Like many others concerned with international relations, Burnett believes that the sovereign national state has become an outdated concept. 'In most of the world it is a mere import from Europe, a conceptual product of European imperialism absolutely disharmonious with the preexisting political culture.'[7] The 'Realist' assumption, or paradigm, is that the typical state in

79

'international society' is that of 19th century Europe, each one maximising power as its main aim.[8] The well-known American exponent of this doctrine, Hans Morgenthau, sees the state as the human being writ large, with similar motives, 'to live, propagate, dominate.' As Burnett says, Morgenthau 'is describing a phenomenon of a very limited historical time and place.'[9] Martin Wight, though, in *Power Politics*, agrees with Morgenthau in assuming that the subject mainly concerns states patterned like the 'great powers' in the 19th century.[10] In Johnston's book, Burnett is pointing out that during the last half-century the basic assumptions about international relations have been changing. Moving beyond the state, there is now 'a need to consider other actors, other influences and motivations, other approaches to negotiation and strategy. And, as the cases show, this *is* emerging, not (yet) as a systematic effort by foreign ministries to achieve greater breadth and effectiveness, but out of the struggle of mankind to find paths out of impasse.'[11]

The aim of governments is not usually power for its own sake, but more likely security, as it often was even in the age of the 19th century 'great powers'. 'In today's world of ethnic strife and high-technology weaponry, orthodox concepts of security based on a competition of armaments will no longer be adequate,' says Johnston. 'Increasingly, security will become a function of the strength and durability of national and international relationships.' As regards 'a new paradigm for international relations, the challenge is to reach beyond the state-centric focus of the power-politics model to accommodate nongovernmental interactions at the subnational and individual levels. The case studies in this book illustrate that there is a distinct role for nongovernmental actors in building and changing relationships through dialogue and conflict resolution processes. The Franco-German initiative with its early contribution to European unity is a particularly compelling example.'[12]

There is a 'general long-term unwillingness to make war'.

With conflicts, there comes a time when the combatants, at least on one side, have had enough and are 'ripe' for a settlement – they realise that no advantage can come out of further struggle. This 'erosion of the willingness to make war' often 'starts with citizens before it reaches governments'.[13] At this stage moves by 'religiously-motivated' groups or individuals may have a decisive effect.

In discussing these matters Burnett prefers the word 'spiritual' – 'Religion', he says, is 'inadequate to express the range of interest.'[14] Johnston, in his Introduction, explains 'the distinction between religious and spiritual phenomena ... *Religion* is meant to imply an institutional framework within which specific theological doctrines and practices are advocated and pursued ... *Spirituality*, on the other hand, transcends the normal parameters of organised religion, suggesting a less bounded and, at times, more far-reaching scope of human involvement.'[15]

Spirituality, Burnett concludes, depends on the acceptance of good rather than bad 'values', 'as we imprecise moderns label it' – the ancients were much better in this respect, realising that 'the character of the citizens and the character of the regime are inextricable'.[16] A great deal depends on the *vision* of those chiefly concerned: 'the character of a conflict is changed when the parties are able to look up, to see larger and loftier consider-ations'[17] (an insight which parallels Monnet's dictum about the importance of 'changing the context'). 'If political leaders and statesmen around the globe are insufficiently broad in their vision and in the people and considerations they are willing to bring to the table, they will be unable to be of much help for most of tomorrow's serious conflicts.'[18]

Burnett has no doubt that 'spiritual factors must ... play an increasing role in the resolution of political conflict because of the absence of an alternative. Marx has fallen of his own insuffi-ciencies ... Nationalism is still very much with us, but it more often intensifies than reduces conflict. Modernity itself does not produce, in the place of a guiding idea system, much beyond material abundance in some places, desperation and envy in others, and economic theories to explain both.'[19]

To revert to Johnston, 'today's model leans heavily on the recycling of old approaches and adapting them to fit new problems, problems which they are ill-designed to accommodate ... There is a need to go beyond the normal mechanisms to uncover and deal with the sources of conflict by rebuilding relationships and making concessionary adjustments wherever possible. In this context, reconciliation born of spiritual conviction can play a critical role by inspiring conflicting parties to move beyond the normal human reaction of responding in kind, of returning violence for violence. And therein lies an extraordinary challenge.'[20]

The way in which the Franco-German conflict was transformed into partnership set a new precedent in conflict resolution. Now there are 'broader agendas' in the policies of states than in former times: questions of welfare become as important as security; there are new 'global values.'[21] 'Human rights' have become important as international issues, while 'transnational religious groups' such as Muslim fundamentalists or political Zionists may play predominant roles. Agendas, norms and paradigms have been constantly changing.

Although a major aim of Johnston's book is to alert professional policy-makers and diplomats to the importance of 'the missing dimension', its focus (notably in the case-studies) is on the part that non-governmental organisations (NGOs) can play in defusing conflicts and helping towards their solution. As Johnston says, 'Nation-state negotiations and the interactions of official diplomats (track I) are consistent with the basic paradigm of international relations set forth by Hans Morgenthau, [but] as illustrated by some of the case-studies in this book there are numerous interactions that also take place at the unofficial track II level, many of them to positive effect.'[22]

This point is developed in *The Psychodynamics of International Relationships,* vol.2,[23] edited by Joseph Montville and others.[24] Montville coined the term *Track II* diplomacy, which he defines 'as informal interaction between influential members of opposing groups with the goal of developing strategies ... in ways favorable to the resolution of the conflict.'[25] In chapter 4 Harold H. Saunders writes of 'the widening influence of private citizens in national policymaking and in the conduct of international relationships.'[26] He uses the word *relationship* to indicate the need for attending to human as well as state dimensions in these matters. 'It makes a difference,' he says, 'whether those engaging in dialogue ... develop a relationship within which they can probe the real fears, concerns, and feelings underlying stated interests ... To date, that kind of understanding has been more possible in nonofficial dialogue ... than in official exchanges.'[27]

Saunders stresses the importance of helping the parties concerned to recognise common interests. 'The manner in which one person approaches another ... may determine how quickly they discover common interests.'[28] Steps in this direction can be taken by *people-to-people diplomacy* or 'getting to know the other side'. He quotes President Eisenhower: 'I like to believe that people in the long run are going to do more to promote peace than are governments.'[29] And in doing this, says Saunders, 'citizens may be more effective if they stop to educate themselves in policy thinking ... A multitude of well-meaning citizens craving new relationships of peace and growth may waste a lot of precious energy if they fail to direct that energy precisely to the goals and objectives that need to be achieved.'[30]

These points are well illustrated in the case-studies in *Religion, the Missing Dimension of Statecraft.* Through meeting on neutral ground in a friendly atmosphere, French and German business men, steelmasters and directors of coalmines, were able to look up, to see 'larger and loftier considerations', to have vision which brought into perspective their common interests, and so encouraged them to work towards that partnership between their countries which led to the creation of the first European Community, by way of the policymaking diplomacy of Jean Monnet and Robert Schuman. Similarly, in the ending of the civil war in Rhodesia and the launching of Zimbabwe, the informal conversations between Prime Minister Ian Smith and the nationalist leader Arthur Kanodereka, arranged by Alec Smith, paved the way for the historic meeting of Smith and Robert Mugabe on the eve of the latter assuming power.

In Nicaragua the essence of the moves to conciliation between the East Coast Indians and the Sandinista government was spiritual, in the sense that the meetings of leaders from various Protestant Churches on the Indian side with Catholics or ex-Catholics representing the Sandinistas, were preceded by times of prayer and readings from the Bible. Most meetings were arranged by a Conciliation Commission, set up for this purpose. Its 'infusion of Christian trustworthiness and hope into the negotiating process created unique opportunities for human contact across a great political gulf. When the gulf appeared insurmountable ... their Christian virtues held out a uniquely spiritual bridge to which both sides frequently resorted.'[31] The Commission's 'religiously impelled perseverance − its mixture of pragmatic message-carrying, peace process maintenance, and fund-raising, together with its constant resort to confession, prayer, and scripture reading − helped link developments in the East Coast issues to the wider framework of peace that emerged in Central America.'

In Nigeria as in Rhodesia, Quaker emissaries provided a much valued means of communication for both sides − 'the sole third party that won the complete trust of both parties in the conflict.'[32] Adam Curle, one of three Quaker conciliators in Nigeria, explained that 'virtually the sole dogma ... of Friends concerns 'that of God in every one'.' This 'divine spark' in each person gives the conciliators and the parties 'a real relationship ... In working for peace I am simply doing what I've sensed is carrying out a normal human function: to realize − make real − the bond between us all.'[33] Supporting the ongoing efforts of Arnold Smith, the Secretary-General of the Commonwealth, and others, the Quaker role 'was not so much peacemaking as the communication gap they filled.' In this way, 'by their presence and availability at critical moments, the Quakers succeeded in opening lines of communication that would have otherwise remained closed.'[34] This was their part, 'however indefinable, in winning the extraordinary peace that prevailed in postwar Nigeria.'[35]

During the Cold War, the part of the Protestant Church in Communist East Germany (the German Democratic Republic) is well documented in the book, as keeping alive people's aspirations for freedom and in preparing the way for ousting the regime and securing reintegration with the Federal Republic of Chancellor Kohl. Another case-study, concerning the Philippines shows the power of the Roman Catholic Church to right wrongs and bring about reconciliation. Building on Vatican II as stressing that 'efforts to eradicate injustice and economic inequality were an integral part of preaching the Gospel,'[36] Cardinal Jaime Sin 'forged a working consensus in the Church on matters relating to peace and justice.'[37] In so doing he projected the Church into a role in relation to the existing Government (in the Philippines that of Marcos) similar to that, under the leadership of Cardinal Wyszynski and Pope John Paul II, in Poland. The Church's denunciation of the election of February 1986, rigged by Marcos to secure his power, was decisive, as was its support of the people in their massed confrontation with the army shortly afterwards — the event which persuaded the American Department of State and President Reagan to withdraw support from Marcos and advise his resignation.

This evolving role of the Catholic Church, from tacitly supporting the existing social and political system to becoming a leading actor for change, is also notable in the Rhodesian civil war. In South Africa, as in the German Democratic Republic, it was the Protestants who led the way. In this role Desmond Tutu showed himself to be an outstanding leader, even before he was appointed Anglican Archbishop of Cape Town. In 1976 he said: 'We are involved in the black liberation struggle because we are also deeply concerned for white liberation. The white man will never be free until the black man is wholly free.'[38]

Apartheid (though not yet called by that name) dated back to the days of British rule, when the Natives Land Act of 1913 made it illegal for blacks to own land except in the 13 percent of South African territory designated as African Reserves. As a policy of 'explicit racism'[39] it was consolidated by the series of laws passed by the government of Daniel Malan from 1948 to 1954, backed by the theology of Abraham Kuyper and other clerics of the Dutch Reformed Church, which 'carefully manipulated biblical references in ... providing the early underpinnings for apartheid.'[40] The tower of Babel story (Genesis 11:1-9) was one of those cited.

The anti-apartheid movement was initiated by black mission churches (which became known as the Mission Church) although part of the white-dominated Dutch Reformed Church. They were followed by English-speaking Churches at a conference in 1949, but it took some years — not until 1982 — for the Mission Church to threaten to withdraw from the DRC unless it abandoned its support for apartheid. A year later the Cape Province Synod declared that the Bible did not justify apartheid, and opened its church services to all races. A general synod of the DRC followed suit with a document which 'effectively rejected apartheid as a legitimate ideology.'[41] By this time Britain and other countries had imposed trade sanctions on South Africa, now followed by the USA — moves which were endorsed by the Pope. F.W. de Klerk, becoming President in 1989, immediately took steps to free Nelson Mandela and repeal the apartheid laws.

De Klerk called for the Churches to make their response. 'The largest representation of black and white churches in South Africa's history was assembled [at Rustenburg] to determine ecumenical guide-lines for the post-apartheid era.' Professor Willie Jonker, a Dutch Reformed theologian, unexpectedly pronounced the religious death-knell of apartheid at the conference: 'I confess before you and before the Lord not only my own sin and guilt, and my personal responsibility for the political, social, economical and structural wrongs that have been done to many of you and the results of which you and our whole community are still suffering from, but vicariously I dare also to do that in the name of the DRC of which I am a member, and for the Afrikaans people as a whole.'[42] With the abolition of the theology which supported it, the whole apartheid system collapsed.

Two conclusions in particular follow from the foregoing. Both the professionals (policymakers and diplomats) and NGOs and private individuals need to educate themselves *thoroughly* about situations of conflict before they attempt to bring solutions. Secondly, they should try not merely to understand the moral and spiritual implications in the conflict, but should be ready themselves to bring their own faith and convictions to the leaders and followers. In this way they can help to demolish the ideological pretensions on which one party and/or the other base the policy and behaviour which maintain the conflict.

At the same time, as Barry Rubin says, 'religion plays its role as an important defining characteristic of politically contending communities.' If religion is not recognised in such cases as 'the prime communal identity', their political controversies (adds Burnett) cannot be properly 'understood, predicted or used positively in conflict resolution.'[43] These considerations apply in the most difficult conflict-ridden situations such as Northern Ireland, ex-Yugoslavia and the Holy Land.

As the case-studies indicate, it is not only knowledge of the situations which is needed. If the 'miracles' such as those referred to by Lord Soames are to occur, there must also be dedicated moral and spiritual preparation by those undertaking to bring answers to the problems. The rigorous training of this kind given by Frank Buchman to those who joined him for three months at

Lake Tahoe in 1940 made possible the miracles at Caux in the immediate postwar years and the consequent new partnership among the West European nations. In Rhodesia this kind of leadership was given by Henry Macnicol, who had been at Tahoe, along with others, notably Alec Smith, whose dynamism stemmed from more recent Christian experience and calling. Similar experience was the background of Church leaders such as Cardinal Sin in the Philippines and Archbishop Tutu in South Africa. Such experience is also part of the Quaker tradition, going back to George Fox and followers like Mary Fisher, who in the difficult conditions of the 17th century, travelled to Adrianople for a meeting with Sultan Mohammed IV.

When revolutionary changes for the better occur, it is because minds as well as hearts have responded to the moral and spiritual challenge. The abandonment of the theological underpinnings of apartheid toppled the ideology itself. Similar dramatic changes in biblical and historical theologies are needed if ever there is to be peace in the Balkans and the Holy Land.

In his conclusion Johnston singles out former Yugoslavia. 'Beyond the functional combinations of tracks I and II diplomacy suggested above, there are added possibilities offered by interfaith dialogue ... Because religion constitutes one of the principal ingredients of ethnic identity among the peoples of the former Yugoslavia, it will undoubtedly be one of the keys to any settlement that eventually emerges'.[44] Since this was written hopes have strengthened that action among leaders of the different faiths, notably the attendance of the Serbian Orthodox bishop, Nikolaj Mrda, and the Catholic archbishop, Cardinal Puljic, at the installation of the Reis-ul-elema, Dr. Mustafa Ceric, heralds the needed changes at the grassroots.[45]

Whoever tries to help the countries concerned along these lines will need a strong faith and determination. Are these qualities likely to be evident in the revolutionary age which lies ahead?

1.Oxford University Press, 1994. Douglas Johnston is the executive vice president and chief operating officer of the Center for Strategic and International Studies, Washington DC, in addition to serving as project director of the Religion and Conflict Resolution Project.

2.Martin Hollis and Steve Smith,op.cit.,59.

3.Johnston,4.

4.Ibid.,5.

5.Stanton Burnett is senior adviser and former director of studies at the Center for Strategic and International Studies,Washington DC.

6.Ibid.,291.

7.Ibid.,298.

8.Hans J. Morgenthau: *Politics among Nations, the Struggle for Power and Place* (3rd edition, New York 1962),33.

9.Johnston,298.

10.Martin Wight: *Power Politics* (Royal Institute of International Affairs and Leicester University, 1978), 26.

11.Johnston,301.

12.Ibid.,333.

13.Ibid.,299

14.Ibid.,286.

15.Ibid.,4.

16.Ibid.,300.

17.Idem.

18.Ibid.,302.

19.Ibid.,302

20.Ibid.,333.

21.Joseph S.Nye,: op.cit.,175,183.

22.Ibid.,326.

23.D.C. Heath and Company/Lexington,Mass.,USA,1991.

24.Joseph Montville is a Senior Associate at the Center for Strategic and International Studies and Director of the Center's Conflict Resolution Project.

25.Ibid.,13.

26.Ibid.,41. Dr. Harold Saunders worked for 20 years (1961-81) at the center of U.S.policy-making on the Middle East and Southwest Asia as a former assistant secretary of state and a member of the National Security Council staff. He was one of the principal architects of the Camp David Accords.

27.Ibid.,43.

28.Ibid.,47.

29.Ibid.,55.

30.Ibid.,67-8.

31.Johnston,84.

32.Ibid.,111.

33.Ibid.,95.

34.Ibid.,107,111.

35.Ibid.,111.

36.Ibid.,164

37.Ibid.,159.

38.Ibid.,189.

39.Ibid.,183.

40.Ibid.,186.

41.Ibid.,195.

42.Ibid.,198.

43.Ibid.,21,287-8.

44.Ibid.,329,330.

45.*An Agenda for Reconciliation Towards the 21st Century,* A report on the International Symposium of the Moral Re-Armament International Conference, Caux, 10-15 August 1996,p.8.

CHAPTER 9

THE REVOLUTION OF OUR TIME

Two books by James Dale Davidson and Lord Rees-Mogg, *The Great Reckoning* (1992) and *The Sovereign Individual* (1997), give some insights as to what is happening with the ongoing Information Revolution. 'The microchip has set in motion what promises to be the third great revolution of human life, comparable in its sweep to the Agricultural Revolution that set history in motion and the Gunpowder Revolution that initiated the great surge of human progress at the end of the fifteenth century.'[1] The authors are right in presenting material and technological changes in human society as largely determining cultural changes, but they may not allow enough influence to what they call 'the basic spiritual forces that move mankind.'[2]

Certainly the Agricultural Revolution changed fundamentally the course of human development. Settled life on the land made possible the transition from tribalism to civilisation, and this new type of society opened the way for a new outlook on life, for new religions. To surmise that the Information Revolution of today is likely to prove a similar turning point in history is intriguing and challenging. The Agricultural Revolution brought in civilisation; is the Information Revolution destined to bring in the next stage of social development to what might be called super-civilisation?

It needs a good deal of imagination to accept that the technological and social changes of today are as drastic as those which our ancestors experienced. At that time, some seven or eight thousand years ago, the savannah and forests where they had been living by hunting, fishing and other forms of food gathering for several hundred millennia, began drying up. The melting of the northern ice-cap had signalled the ending of the last Ice Age and a change to a rainy (pluvial) age, when vast areas, now desert, were fertile prairie inhabited by game of every kind. When this period ended and the rain belt moved further north, tribes living

91

in the newly desiccated areas were faced with extinction. Some tribes in North Africa migrated south to areas where rain still fell; others sought refuge in oases. Yet others descended into the Nile Valley, a jungle territory thick with reeds and scrub. Similar migrations occurred in the areas of Tigris and Euphrates, the Indus Valley, and (in China) the Yellow River *(see map at end of book)*.

Tribes in their new habitats encountered difficulties in pursuing their wandering life as hunters and food-gatherers. There was not enough game and too little edible vegetation for the relatively large number of people in what must have seemed restricted areas. But with the problem there was presented the remedy. The alluvial soil, replenished annually by the flooding rivers, is the most fertile in the world. Drop seeds in, and not one but several crops in a year become possible. Food production was further increased by the invention of irrigation. Permanent settlements developed into villages and then cities, with temples and tombs and other adjuncts of civilisation, together with various arts and crafts.

Eventually people in the civilised areas — a few spots on the world map — made contact with each other. After several millennia the new form of society became standard throughout the globe. International trade began. In the Eastern Mediterranean and the fertile crescent international relations of an embryonic type were developing, when by the 13th century BC the Egyptian and Hittite Empires were in contact with Kassite-dominated Mesopotamia by way of Mitanni and Assyria.

Is the Information Age likely to bring changes in human society as far-reaching and profound? Davidson and Rees-Mogg stop short of predicting that in the coming age a new type of society will develop, as different from civilisation 'as we know it' as civilisation is from primitive tribalism: but this may be the vastness of the needed change if humanity is to escape extinction. Nonetheless the changes they predict will be considerable.

Among others 'microprocessing will subvert and destroy the

92

nation-state, creating new forms of social organisation in the process'.[3] But in long established countries pride and patriotism exert a powerful sway over people. In times of peace it is easy to forget how strong is this 'high form of altruism when compared with lesser loyalties and more parochial interests,' to quote Reinhold Niebuhr. 'The unqualified character of this devotion is the very basis of the nation's power and of the freedom to use the power without moral restraint',[4] to the point where men and women are ready to lay down their lives for it.

The state exists to give the individual protection, say Davidson and Rees-Mogg, but such protection will not be needed by the person who can move himself and his money around — and for this he will have a strong incentive in order to escape 'predatory' taxation whereby some of his wealth would be directed to the less well-off. As for taxation to finance defence, that will prove less necessary. Warfare between the developed states is becoming less likely, since 'the end of the cold war ... was the end of the long period of rising returns to violence. The fall of Communism ... was the outward marker of the most important development in the history of violence over the past five centuries. If our analysis is correct, the organisation of society is bound to reflect the growing diseconomies of scale in the employment of violence.'[5]

But what if the analysis is not correct? For instance the authors have some depressing words to say about China. 'Confucianism seems an outmoded tradition to many modern Chinese, who do not value moderation, who respect force rather than authority, and certainly do not treat others as they would wish to be treated themselves ... China, with all its advancing power, is now a morally backward country compared to Tibet, impoverished and oppressed as the Tibetans are.'[6]

China certainly shows no signs of breaking up into its component parts or city-states — in fact its expressed policy, having regained Hong-Kong, is to reimpose its authority over Taiwan. The rest of the world may need all its powers of defence if it — or at least the United States — finds itself in a stand-off with what looks like another superpower in the making. Have our authors any words of hope that mankind may be able to stave off, and perhaps outlaw for ever, another nuclear war which could end the rule of homo sapiens on the planet, or precipitate what might be a terminal dark age?

A people who have been oppressed and repressed, react, when they are freed from the oppression, by imposing a harsh domination on others. During the 20th century, in South Africa, the Afrikaners, having been oppressed by the British, imposed apartheid with all its penalties on the Africans; and the Jews, oppressed and nearly annihilated in continental Europe, have been oppressing the Palestinians, after gaining power in their country. In South Africa it might be expected that it is now the turn of the Africans to oppress the Whites, but so far 'the forgiveness factor', exemplified in the attitude of Nelson Mandela and Archbishop Tutu, has provided a strong influence against this happening, except to a limited extent. This factor, at work between French and Germans in the postwar years, transformed hereditary hates into partnership. Can one envisage a scenario in which something similar might take place between the Chinese and their former European and Japanese oppressors? Are Davidson and Rees-Mogg too pessimistic, in not taking sufficiently into account the Chinese heritage of philosophy, ethics and religion, while failing to assess the need in the short term for a vigilant defence system?

Two developments in particular of the Information Age are (1) a further speeding of historical change, already going at a breakneck rate by comparison with the long millennia of mankind's infancy, and (2) the Internet bringing all parts of the planet into instantaneous relation with each other. It is now possible for the potential of 'the forgiveness factor' and how it comes into operation to become known and have its effect everywhere before long. But this does not mean that the Orient necessarily becomes culturally and spiritually dependent on the West. It has its own rich heritage of faith, philosophy and ethics.

There is of course Confucius and his teaching, but also his

successor of a century later, Mo Ti or Motse (470-391 BC), besides many other sages and teachers. Mo Ti speaks of the benevolence of 'Heaven', which many modern Chinese philosophers interpret as 'a Being or even a Person with a Will'.[7] He speaks of 'standards', such as the craftsman has for his work and which everyone needs in their behaviour towards others, though only those who are 'human-hearted' have them to the full. These are people who take their standards from imitating Heaven, which 'wants men to love and be profitable to each other, and does not want men to hate and maltreat each other ... because it embraces all in its love of them, embraces all in its benefits to them.'[8] Mo Ti was not concerned only with personal morality — a harmoniously organised community was the aim, of which the essential basis was people with high moral standards. He kept a school for statesmen, and many of his alumni took on this role at various courts in China.

'When we discuss his doctrines of 'universal love' and condemnaton of offensive war, for instance,' says his biographer Y.P. Mei, 'we should bear in mind that when he heard of a case of forthcoming war he actually journeyed to the ambitious ruler and exercised his influence to prevent such a project being carried out ... We are told that he walked ten days and ten nights and had to tear off pieces of his garments to wrap up the sore feet, all for the sake of frustrating a vicious attack upon a small state by a large one.'[9]

China has also been remarkably receptive to foreign religions and ideologies: Buddhism, Christianity, Islam, and in modern times Marxism. With the latter's dereliction elsewhere it may cease to have appeal to China's rulers, as already seems to be the case with the educated elite. Instead the great faiths may again come into the ascendant. And if there is a question as to how this may happen one may remind oneself that the Spirit blows where it lists. In the comparable civilisation of Greece and Rome there was no significant material or technical development to trigger massive cultural change, yet in the first centuries of the Christian era there was a 'resuscitation of the religious sense, which gradually took hold of all classes in society.'[10]Our civilisation is as much in need as that of Rome in its decadence, and we may hope (and pray, if we have the faith to do so) that the same wind of the Spirit may blow in China as for us.

The sovereign individual, as depicted by our authors, is shown as someone mainly concerned with keeping and increasing his money, with little regard to the way the world is going around him, and with a marked dislike of the state's 'facilitated systematic, territorially based predation.'[11] He need not keep himself and his money for long in specific locations. 'Transactions on the Internet or the World Wide Web can be encrypted and will soon be almost impossible for tax collectors to capture. Tax-free money already compounds far faster offshore than onshore funds still subject to the high tax burden imposed by the twentieth-century nation-state. After the turn of the millennium, much of the world's commerce will migrate into cyberspace, a region where governments will have no more dominion than they exercise over the bottom of the sea or the outer planets.'[12]

Though nation-states will break up into their component parts, Switzerland, as the most efficient one will survive, to the advantage of moneyed persons who want to migrate there − the richer they are the better the financial arrangements they can have.

The rich everywhere will become richer − the gap between the wealthy and the less well-off, notably the underclass, will become wider, and the same will apply globally between the haves and the have-nots. In fact this is already happening. 'The conflict between the new cosmopolitan elite of the Information Age and the "information poor"'[13] will intensify. As the latter are a much larger proportion than the well-off in the less-developed countries, with few openings for professional training, basic services may decline there, to the disadvantage of the elite as for everyone else. On the day that the London *Times* carried a review of *The*

Sovereign Individual it also reported on 'the likelihood of 'catastrophic accidents' in African airspace caused by the breakdown of air traffic control systems across the Continent.'[14] The report also indicated deficiencies besides poor training in countries that can be classified as 'information poor' — in matters of air control these are 'poorly maintained equipment and corruption. Large overflight and navigation fees are paid to all African states — a typical flight from Johannesburg to London costs an airline more than £5,000 in such fees, but this money simply vanishes and is clearly not being used to maintain air traffic services.' Unless the Information Revolution brings in absolute moral standards as part of its culture, the benefit of its technical advances will accrue as much to miscreants as millionaires.

The sovereign individual sounds too much like the person enjoying 'the culture of contentment'[15] in J.K. Galbraith's book of that name, whose 'perception of government [is] as an onerous. and unnecessary burden.'[16] The attitudes of the 'contented' person toward taxation are 'powerfully adverse.' In the U.S.A., he points out, 'the controlling contentment ... is now that of the many, not just of the few,' operating 'under the compelling cover of democracy ... of those who, in defense of their social and economic advantage, actually go to the polls.'

There are deep 'theological grounds' for this attitude. 'As you must have faith in God, you must have faith in the system; to some extent the two are identical ... To serve contentment, there were and are three basic requirements. One is [that] there must be a doctrine that offers a feasible presumption against government intervention ... The second, more specific need is to find social justification for the untrammeled, uninhibited pursuit and possession of wealth ... There is need for demonstration that the pursuit of wealth or even less spectacular well-being serves a serious, even grave social purpose ... The third need is to justify a reduced sense of public responsibility for the poor. Those so situated, the members of the functional and socially immobilized underclass, must, in some very real way, be seen as the architects of their own fate.'

Wealthy individuals in any culture have the chance of using their money for philanthropic purposes, others merely for ease and pleasure, or for their hobbies. One of these may be collecting art. In periods of great art like the Renaissance the patronage of a Medici is regarded as laudable. But the tastes of a collector today, like that of a gallery or museum director, may help to debase art as well as lowering the general level of taste and morals. As the philosopher Bosanquet said at the start of the century, 'there is *nothing* which large sections of the educated populace (in all ranks of society) will not believe. There is no absurdity so gross as not to find its able journalistic supporters ... There is nothing so bad in art and literature that it will not be welcomed by an enthusiastic crowd.'[17]

In contrast to the self-centred 'sovereign individual', a benevolent prototype of the new Information elite can be found in George Soros. Having made his millions by shifting his money around with a view to maximising profit, as would be normal with a 'sovereign individual' (even before knocking out government policy with regard to the European Exchange Rate Mechanism – ERM – in Britain), Soros had decided to commit himself to 'fighting evil', and to do this with a fund to help set up open societies in countries which had been 'closed'.[18]

He says: 'Some 15 years ago, when the fund had reached a size of $100 million, and my personal wealth had grown to roughly $25 million, I determined after some reflection that I had enough money. After a great deal of thinking, I came to the conclusion that what really mattered to me was the concept of an open society ... to open up closed societies, help make open societies more viable, and foster a critical mode of thinking.'[19] Having set up a foundation for the purpose, his first success was in the country of his birth, Hungary, as it shook off the shackles of Communism. He has been continuing this good work in various other countries since then.

The Soros example may inspire other wealthy people in the Information Age to commit themselves (in the words of Davidson and Rees-Mogg) to 'a dynamic morality which actively wards off evil ... After a period of slack morality, which is indicative of the end of an era, we will see the awakening of a sterner morality, with more exacting demands ... A reputation for honesty will be an important asset in the cyber-economy ... Thus the twenty-first century may see a return to a Victorian-like emphasis on trust-worthiness and character in an environment no Victorian could have envisioned ... Religion is likely to make an intellectual as well as social comeback, as for the first time in centuries science appears to buttress rather than undermine the belief that human history could be unfolding according to a predestined plan.'[20]

An apt commentary on the possible return from modern subjective and relativist 'values' to Victorian 'virtues' is by Professor Himmelfarb in her *The De-moralization of Society*. If we are fortunate enough to see 'virtues' predominate again in Britain, some familiar trends will be bucked. Compared with what happens to the crime rate today, in the half century from 1857 to 1901 the rate of indictable offences was halved, though population had increased by 14 million.[21]

In this respect the view of the future by Davidson and Rees-Mogg is optimistic. If exacting moral standards return as the norm in the West — still better if this were also to occur elsewhere — our world might well move forward into an era of peace, goodwill and general benevolence. This might be acclaimed as 'the end of history', with more justification than the way in which the phrase has been used by Francis Fukuyama to characterise the present existence of liberal democracy in a number of countries. This type of society, he maintains, best satisfies a major motivating factor among people, for which he borrows a Greek word *thymos*, translated as self-esteem and the desire for recognition.[22]

In his next book (1995), *Trust: the Social Virtues and the*

Creation of Prosperity, trust takes precedence over *thymos* as the key element in human society 'that arises within a community of regular, honest and co-operative behaviour, based on commonly shared norms.'[23] When it begins to break down, as in the United States, trouble ensues. Three years on (1998) he identifies the breakdown as moral: 'trust norms' or 'social capital' have been eroded (we might call it the decline of culture), because, through the sexual revolution, women are no longer economically dependent on men. With the pill and condoms, women can 'have sex' without worrying about the consequences — even the economic consequences if they have a child; either they can have a job — a far higher proportion of women than in earlier times are in work outside the home — while at the same time the men who impregnate them are free from their economic responsibilities. With both parents rarely in the home and the single mother often at work outside, children are no longer brought up to practice the necessary 'social norms'. Fukuyama points out that the situation is much better in Japan, where the traditional nuclear family continues to flourish. He recognises that 'religion does and will have an important role' in confronting 'the massive changes in moral standards' which he dates as beginning in 1967.[24]

These conclusions, as a reviewer said,[25] are trite rather than profound, stopping short as they do before suggesting practical ways whereby religion, or any other factor, could improve the situation. There is a hope that genes may play a corrective part — a hope shared by another Western guru, Paul Kennedy, who thinks that biotechnology 'seems likely to introduce a new historical era'.[26] But, however it happens, 'new thinking and new structures' are needed in Europe, says Kennedy, if it is to play its part in re-ordering the world,[27] while 'the steady and insidious decline' of the United States can only be reversed by 'becoming a different kind of country'.[28]But it is not a matter only of particular countries needing to change: 'global trends are so large as to induce despair', and 'nothing less than the reeducation of humankind' is needed if the habitat and civilisation itself are to be saved.[29]

Something is to be learnt from the ancient world. The inhabitants of the Roman Empire during the peaceful period ushered in by Nerva (96 CE) could not have imagined that within two centuries a Germanic tribe would capture and sack Rome itself. The historian Gibbon, during what seemed an equally civilised age in Europe, the 18th century, could write: 'In the second century of the Christian Aera, the Empire of Rome comprehended the fairest part of the earth, and the most civilized portion of mankind. The frontiers of that extensive monarchy were guarded by ancient renown and disciplined valour. The gentle, but powerful influence of laws and manners had gradually cemented the union of the provinces. Their peaceful inhabitants enjoyed and abused the advantages of wealth and luxury. The image of a free constitution was preserved with decent reverence: the Roman senate appeared to possess the sovereign authority, and devolved on the emperors all the executive powers of government. During a happy period of more than fourscore years, the public adminis-tration was conducted by the virtues and abilities of Nerva, Trajan, Hadrian and the two Antonines.'[30]

This idealised picture of the Empire may have been that of a substantial proportion of the inhabitants, even perhaps of many of the slaves, who are guessed to have made up about half the population. For the contented element it may well have seemed to be the end of history, if they ever thought about such matters. And they were doubtless as much under the illusion of permanence as were most British people regarding *their* Empire at the end of the 19th century.[31]

For these people it was a shattering blow when Alaric captured and sacked Rome (410 CE). St. Jerome, the translator of the Bible into Latin, who had emigrated to Bethlehem, spent days and nights thinking of nothing but the catastrophe − 'who could believe that after being raised up by victories over the whole world Rome should come crashing down?'[32] The response of St. Augustine, in his North African bishopric, was to write *The City of God* proclaiming that the fate of even the greatest states (or 'cities') paled into insignificance alongside the eternal and celestial City – this was the true home, and aiming to attain it was the proper motive for righteous living and care for justice in this world.

In fact the upheavals which were to shake the Mediterranean region and Western Asia did not settle down into a form of equilibrium until the end of the millennium. By that time the Dar-el-Islam, the vast area under Muslim dominance, stretched from Kabul to Cordoba. The successor to the Roman Empire, Byzantium, still held Greece, the Balkans and the northern fringe of the Black Sea. The rest of Europe (apart from Muslim Spain), known as Christendom, represented what was to become eventually 'the West' *(see map at end of book).*

An idealised picture of this historical moment appears in the novel *La Guéniza*,[33] based on letters and other documents found in a secret room of that name in the synagogue of Old Cairo, where they had been deposited from 960 CE to the end of the 13th century. The leading banker and merchant, the Jew Nahray ben Nissim, in Fustat (the predecessor of Cairo), capital of the Fatimid dynasty, undertakes a massive enterprise to save the collapse of the Egypt-based currency with the aid of five friends, a Muslim and his brother from North Africa, a Christian from Italy, and two Jewish colleagues, one based at Arles in the South of France, the other at Aden. The story takes place at the end of the period when peaceful commerce could be carried on throughout the Mediterranean and Near East, only to be disrupted by the Christian incursion into Syria and Palestine, the Crusades.

There are those today, notably Professor Huntington, who think that the coming century will be marked by wars between civilisations. 'National states will remain the most powerful actors in world affairs, but the principal conflicts of global politics will occur between nations and groups of different civilisations ... The fault lines between civilisations will be the battle lines of the future.'[34]Certainly there have been, and will continue to be conflicts which have this character, but they may well be of what Huntington calls the 'micro' kind, between 'adjacent groups' as in ex-Yugoslavia, rather than 'macro', that is 'states from different civilisations [which] compete for relative military and economic power.' An example on the larger scale could be Russians versus the 'Turkic ethnic group,' but an escalation (as might be suggested) of the conflict of America and China over Taiwan into full-scale war is unlikely in the foreseeable future owing to the naval preponderance of the USA in the Pacific. An Islamic war versus the West is scarcely conceivable, for Muslim and partially Muslim countries are divided both within themselves and between themselves, as shown in the long war between Iraq and Iran, in the Gulf War, and in the struggle of the Kurds for independence from their neighbours.

But the professor is right to remind us of the fault line between the Orthodox Christians of Central and Eastern Europe and those of the West, which so complicates attempts to bring peace to the Balkans. This is part of our legacy from the Roman Empire. And in certain respects, both in Europe and the world as a whole, much that is going on is a re-play of post-imperial developments as the legions and their successor Byzantine forces were gradually withdrawn. Today the 'empire', active as a 'hegemony' with political influence through the UN and economic control through multinationals, banks and bodies like the World Trade Organisation, is the Euro-American one, and like its predecessor of Rome is infusing its culture into elites of the various countries throughout the world. Hence the divisions within other civilisations and cultures, between Westernised elites and their following, and those adhering to the older ways − divisions which for instance are so strongly marked in Egypt between those who have received a Western type education (even though in Arabic) and the rest including a militant Islamic element. This

103

situation is reproduced in varying degrees in Algeria and many other parts of Africa and also Asia. Whatever clashes of civilisations there may be in the future are likely to be as muted as that of the thoroughly divided West versus the rest in the period of the Crusades.

As long as human nature remains the same, and humans (like ourselves) have to conduct themselves in situations like those of the past, history will tend to repeat itself, though with differences in time-scale and technical facilities *(see chart at end of book)*. This applies in the Orient as in the West, with parallel or analagous phases in China and Europe: early alluvial civilisations moving into politics with competing and warring states, the more powerful absorbing the weaker, until one imposes its hegemony or empire on the others. Empires in turn decline, migrants or 'barbarians' enter their territories by agreement or force, while internal barbarism appears in the decaying political bodies as culture, law (and its enforcement) weaken. Meanwhile the cultural radiation continues to spread far and wide, just as Greek-type states burgeoned in Central Asia and Greek art forms penetrated China, long after Alexander's ephemeral empire had broken up.

Today Western technical, cultural and political forms have been spreading to the farthest (global) limits, while decay and inner barbarisation are the fate of the Euro-American heartlands, as the states withdraw their armed forces from their colonial domains. A brief period of relative peace and prosperity has succeeded the Roosevelt-Truman-Marshall restoration of order in the West, like the restoration of order in the Hellenic 'world' by Augustus. Such restoration may be repeated in the wake of further disorder resulting from the collapse of Communism and the subsequent ethnic/religious terrorism − a work like that of Constantine, ushering in similar changes of ideology and culture, and leading to one or more new civilisations. If the parallels are sound, with the spiritual and moral factors dominating, the forecast of Davidson and Rees-Mogg of a possible return of Victorian standards and values in the coming Information Age may well prove to be correct.

1.James Dale Davidson and Lord William Rees-Mogg: *The Great Reckoning* (London 1991), 26.
2.Ibid.,448.
3.*The Sovereign Individual* (London 1997), 12.
4.Reinhold Niebuhr: *Moral Man and Immoral Society* (New York 1942),91.
5.*Sovereign Individual*,138.
6.Ibid.,369.
7.E.R.Hughes: *Chinese Philosophy in Classical Times* (London 1954), 45,n2.
8.Ibid.,45.
9.Y.P.Mei: *Motse* (Probsthain, London 1934),47.
10.A.Harnack: *The expansion of Christianity during the first three Centuries* (London 1904),28.
11.*Sovereign Individual*,273.
12.Ibid.,19.
13.Ibid.,278.
14.'Times',8 April 1997.
15.J.K.Galbraith: *The Culture of Contentment* (Penguin,London 1997).
16.Ibid.,147. References to the following quotations from Galbraith are pp.44,10,82,96-7.
17.Bernard Bosanquet: *Some Reflections on the Idea of Decadence* (Bangor 1901),15.
18.George Soros: *Soros on Soros* (Wiley,New York 1995), 122.
19.Ibid.,112.
20.*Sovereign Individual,* 358,369-70; *Great Reckoning*,230.
21.Gertrude Himmelfarb: op.cit., 39.
22.Francis Fukuyama: *The End of History and the Last Man* (New York 1992),64.

23.Ibid.,p.26.

24.F.Fukuyama: *The End of Order* (London 1998),104,110*ff.*

25.Ken Jowitt in *The Times Literary Supplement*,23/1/98.

26.Paul Kennedy: *Preparing for the Twenty-first Century* (London 1993),74.

27.Ibid.,288.

28.Ibid.,311,324.

29.Ibid.,335,339.

30.Edward Gibbon: *The Decline and Fall of the Roman Empire* (London 1776-87),1st para.

31.See F.G.Hutchins: *The Illusion of Permanence, British Imperialism in India* (Princeton 1967).

32.J.N.D.Kelly: *Jerome* (London 1975),304; *The Principal Works of St.Jerome* (Select Library of the Nicene and Post-Nicene Fathers,VI,1893),125.

33.Sylvie Crossman and Michel Gabrysiak: *La Guéniza* (Seuil,Paris 1981). The political and economic background of this novel is authenticated in A.R.Lewis: *Naval Power and Trade in the Mediterranean A.D. 500-1100* (Princeton 1951),169-172.

34.'Foreign Affairs'1993, vol.72,no.3,p.22: S.P. Huntington: 'The clash of civilisations'.

CHAPTER 10

STREAMS OF FAITH

If a return to Victorian virtues is the consequence of the coming of the micro-chip, it could indeed be hailed as a revolution. But otherwise the instantaneous globalising process will merely mean more of the same more quickly: weakening and splintering of nation-states and empires, more for this world's haves at the expense of the increasingly impoverished have-nots. But if at the same time there is a *moral and spiritual* revolution, not only may the threat of disaster for humanity be lifted, but a culture of caring may begin to replace the culture of contentment.

Is this a possibility, even a remote one? As individuals we must do what we can, while expecting, hoping and praying for a movement of the Spirit such as that which not only revolutionised and renewed culture in the decadence of Greece and Rome, but which also operated throughout Eurasia from China to Greece and from Scandinavia to Arabia.

This earlier revolution – a moral and spiritual one – which followed the original Agricultural Revolution, was stimulated by the coming of bronze, the smelting of iron, long-distance road-building and improvements in navigation. It can be called the spiritual crisis of the ancient world *(see chart at end of book)*. Prophets and sages had their visions and insights – though many suffered, their teachings became known through the moral laws which they expounded, such as the Ten Commandments, while their visions of a new kind of humanity became current in parables, legends and chronicles. The visions of Ikhnaton and Zoroaster, the intensity of teaching by such as Confucius and Mo Ti, Moses and Jesus, the Buddha and Socrates, St. Paul and Mohammed – all produced changes in personal lives and in society.

These visions and teachings are about a new form of society – in Christian parlance the kingdom of heaven on earth, and in sociological terms a type of society beyond civilisation 'as we know it'.

'There are men who have done in the spiritual world what Darwin and Pasteur did in the world of nature,' says Sir Richard Livingstone.[1]

> [They have] revealed a new attitude and outlook, and so enabled mankind to live on levels which, without their vision, it could not have reached. These are the prophets and religious teachers, who, with a few words, make revolutions in the spiritual life of mankind.

The view of the French philosopher Henri Bergson is that these 'prophets and religious teachers' do not merely forecast through vision and prophecy a higher level of life for their people or for mankind, but that by actually *living* this new way of life they represent *the new type of personality* which the higher level of life will necessitate. This is what he means when, with a graphic figure of speech, he describes them as members of 'a new species'.

> Just as men of genius have been found to push back the bounds of the human intelligence ... so there have arisen privileged souls who felt themselves related to all souls, and who ... were borne on a great surge of love towards humanity in general. The appearance of each one was like the creation of a new species, composed of one single individual. Each one of these souls has marked the attainment of a certain point in the evolution of life; and each of them has manifested in an original form a love which seems to be the very essence of the creative effort ... It is these men who draw us towards an ideal society.[2]

The prophet has sometimes been a voice crying in the wilderness, but more often he becomes surrounded by a band of followers. In this case the group as a whole set themselves to live out the relations which would be normal in the society they are striving to create.

The 'calling' of the creative pioneer continues to impel him to bring about in others the same mutation (to borrow a word from biology) which has happened in himself. Creative personalities 'cannot live and die unto themselves ... Having been lifted up they cannot rest until they have drawn all men unto them; because it is for this that they have come into the world ... They must bring about in their milieu the mutation which they have achieved in themselves.'[3]

The role of the pioneer is thus to bring into being other members of 'the new species', so forming the nucleus of *a new type of society*. This, besides being a working-model of a possible future society, is also the leaven in the lump, orienting society in a direction in which the creative spirit may have fuller play. It becomes the creative minority for society as a whole. The vision has been proclaimed by religious leaders and innovators down the ages – the vision of a new type of world-society: an order that is as different from 'civilisation', as civilisation is different from primitive savagery.

One aspect of the work of the creative pioneers and the minority around them is in fact destructive, tearing down so that better can be built. Their own unconventionality and flouting of norms of behaviour is not merely the expression of the spirit which they feel in their hearts: it is also a deliberate challenge to a world which is hidebound by the shackles of custom and tradition. Some pioneers have gone further than others in challenging the conventions of their day. One of the most extreme cases is that of George Fox, who, with his 'minority' of early Friends (Quakers), challenged the most universally accepted and apparently harmless conventions such as raising the hat as a mark of respect.

If in the West a moral and spiritual ideology is to appear as part of the new Information Society, it will surely be the product

of the three 'streams' from which came the major act of statesmanship of the century, the transformation of French/German
hereditary hostility into partnership. These streams represent those
spiritual societies which may be regarded as the radical exponents
of their faith, looking to the coming of a new order of society or
a better world – streams whose sources in the Renais-
sance/Reformation period (or even before) are to be found in
Quietists and Anabaptists (represented in England by the Quakers
among others), on the Continent by the Catholic saints of the 16th
and 17th centuries, and overseas by the American endeavour
springing from the missions sent out from Halle to the German
and Swiss colonists of Pennsylvania.

Davidson and Rees-Mogg make much of the Renais-
sance/Reformation period which they take as the first phase
following the Gunpowder Revolution. The invention of gunpowder
was obviously important in ending the epoch of feudalism in
Western Europe with its code of chivalry – all the elements of
Medieval culture which declined or disappeared as the Middle
Ages waned. Gunpowder brought about the end of Byzantium
when a cannon (forged by a Dane or Hungarian) breached the
walls of Constantinople in 1453, and it changed the techniques of
warfare and the social conditions on which they were based. But
equally important was the religious, philosophical and scientific
heritage from Greece coming from fleeing Byzantine scholars, and
the scholars from other parts of Europe who drew on the intellectual treasury of Muslim Spain and North Africa. Also printing
from movable type initiated a communications revolution akin to
that of the microchip today. Perspectives changed and possibilities
widened with the voyages of discovery.

Renaissance and Reformation (the two cannot really be
separated) owed their origins to the spiritual upsurge which began
during the first century CE in the Roman Empire. There were no
material or technological changes at the time to explain this
'resuscitation of the religious sense'.[4] Rostovtzeff, in his

magisterial *Social and Economic History of the Roman Empire*, calls for 'a further investigation of this change of mentality ... one of the most potent factors ... in the rise of a new conception of the world and of a new civilisation.'[5] The doyen of Church historians at the turn of the century, Adolf Harnack, writes of 'a veritable revolution to overthrow polytheism and to set up the majesty of God and goodness in the world, [with] a real demand for purity, consolation, expiation and healing.'[6]

Among all the religions coming from the Orient, Christianity impressed the most by demonstrating on a hitherto undreamed of scale the way in which men and women could care for each other, with a thorough-going service of help for the sick and for those otherwise in need, besides extending this aid to pagans.

Its part in the re-moralising of society was impressive, not only by the way in which ordinary people lived the Gospel teaching in their daily life, but also because they were prepared to suffer very cruel martyrdoms under persecution. 'For over a century and a half,' says Harnack, the Church 'ranked everything almost secondary to the supreme task of maintaining its morality.'[7]

Such an array of remarkable and often attractive figures was nurtured by Christianity, both men and women, that it is not surprising that eventually it became the generally accepted faith in the Empire and its successors. Mostly it is the men who get into the history books, and what astonishing personalities many of them were. As society slid further into decadence in the second and third centuries, leadership not only in cultural life but also in politics was moving increasingly towards men like Athanasius of Alexandria with his friend of the desert, St. Antony; to St.Basil, with his brothers and sister Macrina, establishing a huge complex of two hospitals, a hospice and workshops at Cappadocian Caesaraea in Asia Minor (present-day Turkey); Augustine, who like Basil had given up an academic career to minister to his fellow-countrymen and became the greatest thinker to bridge the frontiers between the old civilisation and the new; and great popes, notably Leo and Gregory — Leo who saved Rome from Attila and protected it from the worst barbarity of Genseric, and Gregory who virtually ruled Rome a century later, bringing to his work the best professionalism of the now defunct Empire in the West, and enabling the city to be provisioned (with the aid of dedicated women). He averted the hostility of the Lombards, while keeping a link with the Emperor at Constantinople — he also found time to despatch a mission to christianise England.

Constantinople had been established by Constantine over a century before, at the time when he was making Christianity the official faith of the Empire. The Council over which he presided at his Balkan palace in Nicaea put the faith on a sound doctrinal basis which has lasted until modern times. These were acts of consummate statesmanship, matched in the economic sphere by fixing the solidus, the standard unit of currency, at 4.48 grammes of gold, which maintained its value, to the benefit of Mediterranean trade, for a thousand years. The spiritual upsurge which had brought the Church to its dominant position had meanwhile transformed culture at every level — had in fact created two new civilisations, Byzantine and Western.

The formative influences which this spiritual revolution developed had originated several centuries before at the very basis of society, that is marriage and the family, when the 'great age' of Greece had ended with the long-drawn war between Athens and Sparta. In the Hellenistic Age that followed, new ways, new life coexisted with the decadence — a constant feature in the transitions of civilisation — particularly as intimacy came to replace formality in the lives of married couples, and affection or even love appeared as a motive for matrimony alongside the old intention of maintaining the family lineage (not that girls had any more say in the matter than they had in the old dispensation). The upper classes in Rome were more progressive than the Athenians in educating girls beyond a knowledge of the household necessities, and in giving wives a higher status as partners. Stoicism, which for some educated people was as much a faith as a philosophy, along with religions from the Orient, notably Judaism and Christianity, strengthened the marriage bond and improved the upbringing of children.

These changes were reflected in literature, with novels becoming a popular medium, while the first intimate autobiography – in the form of a prayer – appeared with Augustine's *Confessions*. In art, mosaic took precedence over sculpture, showing its full glory of Christian themes in the mausoleum of Empress Galla Placidia and the churches of Ravenna, while the dome, which had shown its possibilities in the Pantheon at Rome, was developed to a high degree in that triumph of architecture, Hagia Sophia, at Constantinople. In the following centuries the superb romanesque style became traditional for churches throughout Europe.

As important as new writing was the transmission of the old. A landmark in this was the founding of a monastic college and library by the retired civil servant Cassiodorus on his estate in Southern Italy, a century after the Western Empire fell. There, and in the scriptoria of monasteries in the West and of Byzantium in the East, the good work of copying ancient texts, along with the Bible and Christian writings, continued throughout the Middle Ages.

The reason why the monastic movement, especially under the Rule of St. Benedict, had such a positive effect on the burgeoning civilisation of Christendom ('the West') was the way it generated spiritual power among sizeable groups of people. To abandon 'the world' at the time (end of the 4th century) as Benedict did, coming from a privileged and comfortable home, was a sacrificial act. In Italy the peace was still holding which had been re-established by the German generals who had taken over when the last official emperor was pensioned off in 476 CE. It continued to be ruled with the aid of the old professional families, to one of which Benedict belonged. With his education and background he

113

could have expected a promising and agreeable career in the Ostrogothic state, but all these advantages had to be rejected as too much part of a society whose values and morals had not yet changed under Christian influence to the point where they were acceptable to a young idealist. Leaving home when still a teenager, he managed to stand the rigours, physical and psychological, of a lonely life in the wilds of Subiaco, the grounds of one of Nero's deserted palaces. Resisting the usual temptations – he nearly abandoned his retreat for a girl who had previously attracted him – he persisted, helped by another hermit nearby from his meagre store of food. Before long other young men came to join him, so forming the live cell of a movement which was to spread throughout Western Europe, effecting, it has been claimed, 'a revolution in the moral attitude of man'.[8] One woman in particular had a part in Benedict's achievement, his twin sister, Scholastica, who founded a convent near his monastery – a kind of partnership, though they allowed themselves only one meeting a year.

This was the work of the Church in the so-called Dark and Middle Ages. Benedict's success came from 'linking on Monasticism with labour.' The inspiration given to the movement by his *Rule* 'would have been of little value, at any rate viewed from the standpoint of social development, had it not been accompanied by the glorification and systematization of toil.'[9] It shifted the motivation for a dedicated Christian life from the aim of self-mastery by austerity to work – gardening and doing the chores – as well as prayer, worship and study, with care for others, to take up the energies of mind and body. When Duke Godfrey of Lorraine found his brother Frederick washing dishes in the monastery kitchen and told him sarcastically that it was a fine occupation for a count, he replied 'You are right. I ought indeed to think myself honoured by the smallest service for the Master.'[10] This aspect of work-ethic appeared after many centuries, with husbands ready to do such household chores, as an almost unique feature of Western civilisation.

As the Middle Ages waned and the Church's authority diminished, another spiritual upsurge began with the Renaissance and Reformation. This was largely a Western development − the Church had split in 1054, and its Eastern (Orthodox) part had been weakened by the advance of Islam, while the Tatar occupation of most of Russia retarded its evolution by several centuries. With the Reformation in Western Europe the norms of spirituality and moral standards which the Church had stood for in its earlier centuries were restored. While Lutheran and other breakaway Churches burgeoned in the 16th and 17th centuries, the Mother Church reformed herself in terms of doctrine and order through the Council of Trent (1545-63). Equally, or more important in this respect, were the saints who re-invigorated the Church at the grassroots.

Philip Neri, as a young Florentine in Rome, studied in austere conditions and was ordained, making his name by the original ways in which he brought the Christian life to the younger generation, with simple services and hymns in Italian (not Latin) − a kind of 'top of the pops' − which blossomed, after transfer to a specially built room called the Oratory, into plays and other musical entertainments (hence 'oratorio'). An aristocratic but equally effective saint was St.Francis de Sales (the chateau of his birth), bishop of Geneva at an early age, but located at Annecy because Calvin had taken over the city and cathedral. He was a famous preacher who declined a court position at Paris, ordering his days in such a way as to be available for his own townsfolk 'like a fountain in the market-place'. Like Philip Neri he encouraged plays with a Christian message. In his highly influential *Introduction to a Devout Life* he says 'we must if possible avoid making our devotion a nuisance' and suggests 'an hour every day, some time before the midday meal, in meditation, and the earlier the better, because then your mind will be less distracted, and fresh after a night's sleep; but do not spend more than an hour unless your spiritual director expressly tells you to do so.'[11]

A well-known Catholic saint whose life overlapped with the other two, is Vincent de Paul. Captured by pirates as a young man, he escaped, and gave his life in France as a priest, devoted to helping the sick, prisoners and galley-slaves — he was appointed almoner-general of the galleys. He also founded the Priests of the Mission, an association based at St. Lazare in Paris, which did essential work in helping parish priests in their duties. Another was Ignatius Loyola, who — as a Spanish professional soldier recovering from serious wounds — read a book, *The Lives of the Saints*, which was the first step towards transforming him into the founder of the most effective educational and missionary body of the day, the Society of Jesus, known as Jesuits.

Less well-known, but equally remarkable, was Bartolomé de Las Casas, who sailed with Columbus on his third voyage to the West Indies, and after further voyages there, as an ordained priest strove valiantly to reduce the horrors of ill-treatment by the Spanish colonists of the native people. But as this continued, to prevent their extermination he supported the policy of bringing African slaves in their place, though bitterly repenting this advice when he witnessed similar sufferings being inflicted on *them* — never ceasing, into his nineties, to strive on their behalf with successive kings of Spain and the other authorities.

The tradition of radical Catholicism continued in France into the 18th century with Archbishop Fénelon (1651-1715) and his good works at Cambrai. Christian endeavour thereafter in the century was eclipsed by Voltaire, Rousseau and others who devoted their lives to spreading ideas and militating for justice (as in the case of Jean Calas) from a deist or agnostic standpoint. But after the years of Revolution it surfaced again with Félicité de Lamennais, who with his friends Lacordaire and Montalembert vainly tried to convert Pope Gregory XVI to the virtues of freedom — of the press, of conscience and association. His *Paroles d'un croyant*, which he wrote after this experience was a cry from the heart which even stopped the printers as they paused to discuss it while setting up the type. To a public brought up on Voltaire, Diderot and other exponents of Enlightenment teaching, the apocalyptic, prophetic note was new and disturbing. His call for social justice rings out — he supported striking workers and other forms of action against oppression.

Lacordaire made his name with courses which he gave at the Collège St.Stanislas in Paris. Its Director was Alphonse Gratry, whose vision was 'to lift up the world, the family, the entire human race, to a truer life such as the Gospel brings.' He believed that the Gospel shows a way or 'science' for transforming society. 'Life, time and money' had to be dedicated 'to suppress evils which lead to poverty, hunger and death' — evils such as 'men dying of hunger in the midst of cities gleaming with luxuries, their corpses, together with the refuse of last night's orgies, exposed at the doorsteps of houses.'[12]

Perturbed about the situation in Europe as the Crimean War came on, he appealed for a Christian nation to set its course 'for peace and not war as the honour and glory of peoples'[13] ... For this,'supernatural strength' was needed. 'The Master says: Change yourselves ... a radical change, a transformation.'[14] The way to go about this is to listen to God, who is speaking by the inner voice to everyone. In order to listen we must be quiet, and victory must be won over 'the inner talkativeness of empty thoughts, restless desires and entrenched prejudices..What does it actually mean to listen to God? Here is the answer: You will write ... You must take your pen ... just write, in a few words, the naked and unadorned truth ... When the soul meditates quietly and hears something from God, peace and joy flood in.' [15]

For some years after Gratry resigned, the College continued to propagate his ideas. A later student was Marc Sangnier, who had been introduced by his grandmother to Gratry's *Les Sources*. Stirred by the conviction 'of a great task to accomplish — to bring about the coming of God's reign on earth,'[16] he started a well attended lunch-break discussion group. Friends published a paper, *Le Sillon*, which gave its name to a party within the growing Christian-Democratic movement. Despite opposition from Rome to the paper, re-named *l'Avenir*, the party continued to flourish, supporting reforms such as arrangements in industry for workers' participation in management.

The war in 1914 took Sangnier to the front. He survived to sit in the postwar Assembly (Parliament) where he was often a lone voice, castigating the self-contradictory policy of suppressing Germany while exacting huge sums in reparations, instead of promoting the construction of a peaceful Europe. On his estate he organised meetings, courses, concerts and plays (an open-air theatre was built) designed particularly to attract young people, including Germans. Three aircraft hangars end-to-end could hold 20,000 for special meetings.

Sangnier's brand of radicalism eventually found its political expression in the Parti democrate populaire (PDP) formed by some of his followers in 1924, which was joined by Robert Schuman in 1931. The old *Sillon* premises were used as a Resistance base during the German occupation 1940-45, after which the party's name was changed to Mouvement républicain populaire (MRP), attracting a third of the vote at the polls in October 1945. Schuman was one of those elected on the MRP ticket.

At the Reformation radical Protestants were often called Anabaptists and sometimes Quietists. The Quietists' concern was for personal change and seeking the 'inner light' of God's guidance, with meetings for prayer and Bible-study. They believed that the indwelling Spirit of Christ could perfect a person's nature – this was the real change, the essential revolution, all else, including the form in which those called of God should meet or worship being secondary. With the name of Pietists in Germany and movements like the Quakers in England, they formed a parallel stream to that of the radical Catholics, flowing from the common source in the Renaissance, sometimes undergound, but welling up to provide the dynamism and mystique for effective action at crucial moments in society and politics. With little interest in dogma, an emphasis on 'heart' rather than 'head', and an openness regarding ritual and church order, they were the pioneers of ecumenism.

Their spirit infused the political aspects of English Puritanism, and later had a large part in inspiring the Wesley brothers and other initiators of the evangelical movement in Britain. The works of one of the leading German Pietists, August Francke, were highly esteemed by the Wesley parents in their impoverished rectory, and *True Christianity* by Johann Arndt (1555-1621) became a cherished book for the Alsatian philosopher Albert Schweitzer (1875-1965), love for it being passed on to him by his mother.

Francke (1663-1727) took an outstanding part in the German renewal movement stemming from Pietism, making the newly founded University of Halle in Saxony the main disseminating point for Pietism in Europe and America. His astonishing energy in creating educational and charitable institutions, as well as a press and publishing house, was matched by his influence on Count Zinzendorf, the revitaliser of the Moravians, and on Henry Muhlenberg, most prominent of those pastors who were sent from Halle to America, from the mid-18th century onwards, at the request of German-speaking colonists there. This was the beginning of a third 'stream' issuing from the Renaissance/Reformation: Anglo-American evangelism, in which Britain, through John Wesley (the decisive moment of whose change came through the Moravians), had a large part.

Of all the 'creative minorities' which brought change to Britain as the 19th century opened, none were more effective than the so-called Clapham Sect of William Wilberforce and his friends and relatives. They regarded themselves as 'part of a large united family', with all the easy informality of close kinship, living in each others' homes, several of which were at Clapham, then a leafy village three miles from London. In their campaigning to abolish the slave trade and eventually slavery itself, and in promoting other notable reforms — including Wilberforce's great aim of reviving Christian morals and manners throughout the land — 'they assembled as frequently as possible to breakfast at each other's houses, or to discuss plans far into the night.'[17] They worked together on documents and evidence, making out their case for presentation in Parliament or publication in various forms, and in so doing pioneered modern methods of propaganda with pamphlets, lectures, press articles and posters. In these campaigns women took a major part, opening the way to their eventual full participation in public life. Much resulted from interviews with leading figures which, in the case of Wilberforce, were often planned not merely to gain a supporter but to win the man, Prime Minister or peer or whoever he might be, to a faith as radiant as his own.

The third stream, coming to Europe by way of America, was characterised by the proliferation of Churches, sects and all kinds of associations such as those which the Pilgrim Fathers and other immigrants brought with them. The fact that the frontier of settlement was being pressed ever further westwards encouraged the notion that the frontier of Christendom could be extended by spreading the Gospel throughout the world 'as the waters cover the sea'. Missionary enterprise was stimulated on a scale never seen before, notably in China, with a degree of protection and well-developed transport and communications, under the aegis of the Euro-American hegemony.

In evangelising endeavour there was a close connection between Britain and America going back to colonial times. Besides Wesley many other British had an immense impact on America, and from America came Moody and Sankey. Their mission to Britain of 1873-4 reinvigorated the faith of many and made a multitude of new converts.

Among those who responded was Henry Drummond, then a student at Glasgow, impressed by the preaching but more by the after-work, when he was drawn into helping men who came to the 'inquiry room'. Later, when Professor of Natural Science at the Free Church College at Glasgow, he made his mark not only as a teacher, but through his writings in which he expressed his Christian ideals in terms of the still novel doctrine of evolution and of his own scientific findings. His weekly meetings for students in which he expounded these truths with great clarity and a strong challenge, were filled to capacity. On visits to the USA, mainly for speaking engagements on the campuses, he worked with Moody who started summer conferences on his estate at Northfield, Connecticut, after the encouraging response (despite initial rowdyism) to a mission at Oxford and Cambridge.

With Drummond there is a reaching out to the world. Visiting China, he saw the vast needs of a sub-continent whose civilisation was disintegrating, and realised that if anything significant were to be done it could not be left to each individual working on his own. A strategy was needed.

A sense of strategy became one of the distinctive marks of the Anglo-American campus movement, along with a concern that decisions by people to change their way of life should lead to a full commitment. The conviction of the leadership was that effective strategies could be found through openness to God's guidance. The warrant for this was to be found in St. Paul who had set his heart on bringing his message to Rome — though at the same time he was open to other leadings whose strategic implications might not seem so obvious, as in responding to the call to Macedonia. In later days a similar sense of strategy had been shown by Gregory the Great in directing missions to the various tribes of the Empire's invaders.

Besides Moody's Northfield conferences, a major influence on the American campuses was the Young Men's Christian Association — another instance of British initiative finding large fulfilment in America. It was started by George Williams in 1844, growing from a prayer-meeting of twelve men in a London drapery business where he worked. Besides providing educational and social facilities, it was a strongly evangelical body, and the evangelical aim dominated the numerous branches of the Student YMCA in America.

It provided a forum for visitors like Kynaston Studd, a well-known British cricketer. Having been invited by Moody to tour American campuses, Studd at Cornell encouraged the student leader John R. Mott to devote himself to the work in which he was to be the leading figure for two generations. Mott became a moving force on the campus in 'decisive, life-changing work of a permanent character'.[18] He was put in charge of all the student work in North America under YMCA auspices, and in 1886 attended Moody's 'summer school', when a hundred students came forward to form the nucleus of the Student Volunteer Movement which later developed into the World's Student Christian Federation.

For Mott students were 'strategically the most important group in the world', and he saw their task in military terms − 'an army of well-furnished God-called volunteers', and spoke of battlefields and forts.[19] One of his books was *Strategic Points in the World's Conquest*. His primary aim was 'not to get great numbers of men, but to get the ablest strongest men, those who in any walk of life would be leaders', and he quoted Drummond: 'if you fish for eels you catch eels; if you fish for salmon you catch salmon.' So clear was he on his priorities that on one occasion he declined an invitation to meet Kaiser Wilhelm II of Germany because it would have jeopardised his engagements with students, and he refused the pleadings of the American President Woodrow Wilson to accept the embassy in China.

In 1910 Mott chaired the great missionary conference in Edinburgh, where practically all denominations except the Roman Catholic were represented − a conference which sought to realise the vision of the 18th century missionary pioneer, William Carey, for planning unitedly to bring the Gospel to the world.

Mott's watchword was 'the evangelising of the world in this generation' — not that this meant an intention to convert everyone, but 'to give every person of this age an opportunity to accept Jesus Christ.' A millenarian note is evident: the changes consequent on this action at this 'decisive hour of the world's history' would be 'the enthroning of Christ in the individual life, in family life, in social life, in national life, in international relations, in every relationship of mankind.'[20]

The vision was broad and general, with no specific strategy for ending particular social evils in the way that Wilberforce and his Clapham friends had set themselves to abolish the slave trade and slavery, or Lord Shaftesbury had led the country and Parliament in abolishing child-labour and reducing working hours in mines and factories. Though 'the social gospel' did in fact have a powerful appeal for many Americans, for Mott the concern was primarily for a new international order. Converting students on the scale he had in view was, he maintained, 'helping to unite the nations by stronger and more enduring bonds than arbitration treaties, because it is fusing together by the omnipotent Spirit of Christ the students who are to be the leaders of nations.' National distinctions were being eroded within the federation he created — among its students 'there is no Britain and no America, no France and no Germany, no China and no Japan, but Christ is all in all.'[21]

Mott carried his message to British campuses with considerable effect. He spoke to crowded meetings — it was reckoned during a week in 1908 at Oxford that almost the entire student body of 3,000 attended, with three lectures for dons, a meeting for women, and at the conclusion a closed gathering of 230 men 'selected from the 21 colleges with reference to their powers of leadership.' The Muslim students were not neglected — he had a breakfast with them, while the rowing men and other sportsmen gave him lunch at Vincent's. During this visit a 'large number' of undergraduates requested interviews.[22]

In later life such personal encounters might tend to be squeezed out by public occasions and committees, but there were others with whom Mott worked who had made a science or 'art'of 'soul-surgery'. At Yale Henry B. Wright — who also came to his Christian commitment through Moody's Northfield conferences — developed new approaches to students culminating in his book *The Will of God and a Man's Life Work*, a study course in 26 lessons. 'God has a plan for every human life,' he wrote.[23] 'God has a plan for the development of the world which extends to all departments of life and to all spheres of human activity.' After teaching Classics for some years, a special Chair of Christian Methods was created for him. He and his wife set up their home near the campus in order to provide a convenient haven of hospitality. His period of prayer and Bible study before breakfast was the secret of his effectiveness, but he also kept his mind alert during the day for 'luminous thoughts', which he jotted down in a notebook to be acted upon at the appropriate time. He treated these impulses with respect, for he was convinced that through such thoughts God could guide a person in his life and calling, if 'the receiving instrument' was kept clean.[24]

In this context he quoted another Northfield recruit, Robert Speer, who in his book *The Principles of Jesus* set forth the four 'absolute standards of Jesus ... No man who through the deliberate act of surrender of the human will to absolute standards of purity, honesty, unselfishness and love, has once felt the coursing of these immortal powers in his spirit, can ever after find any experience of this new life tame or commonplace.'[25]

To men of Mott's convictions the war of 1914-18 came as a fearful shock. They had been relying on the apparently secure world framework of law and order organised and dominated by Europe, in which to operate for carrying out their evangelising task. Now that order had been shattered, and, among other consequences, Russia — in extent and potentiality one of the

124

greatest fields for this endeavour – had been withdrawn into the camp of militant atheism. The war also shattered 'the easy, optimistic complacency', as Sherwood Eddy, one of Mott's fellow-workers put it, 'of a fictitious evolutionary social development towards millennial utopias.'[26] Mott was disconcerted by 'the frightful moral collapse' occasioned by the war, while the YMCA, which had been the main vehicle of his work, was no longer in the running to repair the evil. Having devoted itself to welfare for the troops, it became in peace-time, with its hostels and similar services, an unrevolutionary part of the system.

Though Mott lived on until 1955, concerned mainly with the ecumenical movement, his mantle in respect of his wider work with students and statesmen fell upon Frank Buchman. Buchman was remarkable not only for the way in which he developed the 'art' of changing lives and encouraging commitment particularly among the younger generation, but for the strengthening of his conviction as the world crisis deepened, that a *strategic* approach was needed if humanity was to be 'turned God-ward' and civilisation saved – a strategy which was for 'everyone every-where', going well beyond winning students as the vanguard of the new age. This conviction and his faith in the unlimited possibilities in every person, led eventually to a strategy for contributing to the resurgence of Western Europe, and of Japan among other countries.

If Buchman was optimistic about individuals, he did not share the illusions of the pre-1914 years that the spread of Christianity by itself would lead to the solution of world problems. Christianity would only be effective, he believed, if its challenge reached right down to the root motivations of individual lives, in matters of sex and the desire for security, and in the urge to gain power and control over others. Further, the number of people so changed would have to be considerable if mankind was to follow another way than 'its historic road to violence and destruction.'[27]

As a young man Buchman's Christian commitment had never

been in doubt, but it was his experience of the Cross at Keswick in 1908, and his subsequent decision to devote the first hour of each day to quiet awareness of God and listening to Him, that brought him to spiritual leadership. This was developed by six years of 'laboratory time' at Pennsylvania State College. In 1915 he went to India to help in the mission to students under YMCA auspices. His work there convinced him that the mass approach was unproductive, like 'hunting rabbits with a brass band.' Progress would only come by 'dealing individually with men.'

His vision was enhanced by his time in China, at a period when leading personalities such as the American-educated Sun Yat-sen were more open to Western infuences than ever before or since. Sun had been the first President of China after the Manchu Empire fell in 1911, and though his power had waned amidst the increasing anarchy, there seemed to be a chance that he or his associates, who were mostly Christians at any rate in name, could be inspired to undertake a work of spiritual reform and so provide the moral infrastructure for the nation.

It was a strategy which went far beyond the thinking of most missionaries in the field. Though the immediate outcome was disappointing, due in part to the opposition of European missionaries who were challenged in their comfortable assumptions and personal shortcomings, Buchman never lost his vision of 'world-changing through life-changing.' The friendships he made during his travels, such as with Mahatma Gandhi and, in Japan, Viscount Shibusawa (one of the pioneers of the Meiji Revolution) continued in the following generations with their children and grandchildren.

Meanwhile he continued to build up his 'force' or team, mostly from undergraduates and graduates of Princeton and Oxford, besides other universities on both sides of the Atlantic – a team which, before long increased to include men and women from all walks of life and most nationalities around the world.

Such were the streams which flowed together, originally from Greece and the Orient, by way of Rome, Byzantium and Muslim

Spain, eventually through post-Renaissance Europe and America to their confluence in the West, inspiring the historic step of creating partnership among the previously warring nations. Can such another giant stride be taken, bringing peace and harmony to a world of vast potential for humanity, as the alternative to violence and destruction? These are also the streams which can supply the personal needs of all those who seek vision and dynamism for the decades and centuries to come.

1.Sir Richard Livingstone: *Education for a World Adrift* (Cambridge 1945),65.

2.Henri Bergson: *The two Sources of Morality and Religion* (Eng.trans.London 1935),77,96-7,54.

3.A.J.Toynbee: *A Study of History* (Oxford 1935),III,236.

4.Harnack,op.cit.,I,28.

5.M. Rostovtzeff: *Social and Economic History of the Roman Empire* (Oxford 1957),540.

6.Harnack,op.cit.,I,118.

7.Harnack: I,258,487-8.

8.H.B.Workman: *The Evolution of the Monastic Ideal* (London 1913 and 1927),154.

9.Ibid.,219.

10.Ibid.,156.

11.St.Francis de Sales: *Introduction to the Devout Life* (London 1956), 52.

12.Alphonse Gratry: *Meditations (London 1889), 89.*

13.Gratry: *Philosophie de la connaissance de Dieu* (Paris 1856), II,491.

14.Ibid.,II,182.

15.Gratry: *Les Sources* (Paris 1876), ch.1;ch.2,36.

16.Marc Sangnier: *Autrefois* (Paris 1936), 182.

17.Viscountess Knutsford: *Life and Letters of Zachary Macaulay* (London 1900) I,253.

18.Basil Matthews: *John R. Mott* (London 1934), 107.

19.Ibid.,441.

20.John R.Mott:*The Evangelisation of the World in this Generation* (London n.d.?1901),16.

21.Matthews,344.

22.John R. Mott: *Addresses and Papers* (New York 1946), I:18; II:4,5.

23.Henry B.Wright: *The Will of God and a Man's Life Work* (New York 1924).

24.George Stewart: *Life of Henry B.Wright* (New York 1925),72.

25.Robert E.Speer: *The Principles of Jesus* (New York 1902).

26.Sherwood Eddy: *A Pilgrimage of Ideas* (New York 1935),16.

27.Buchman, op.cit.,38.

CHAPTER 11

STOP-GO IN SPIRITUAL PROGRESS

Spiritual streams may flow for centuries, but the people whom they inspire are subject to the usual ups and downs in their experience and dedication. Great movements of faith initiate and mould cultures, but whatever development there may be cannot be charted as a steadily rising graph. The tempo and challenge of change cannot be sustained: most people cannot live continuously in a revolution, and revert to 'living and partly living'.[1] There is a falling-away, perhaps a rejection of the new faith or ideology; or if not an outright rejection, a lifeless copy of the new modes with dogmas which are but the husks of former convictions. Meetings of the faithful are organised in temples, chapels or churches (in the case of Communist apparatchiks in uninspiring conference rooms).

Church religion, and similar phases of faith or ideology (no matter what kind of meeting places there are), and the corresponding rituals, have their part in strengthening society – are part of the cement preventing breakdown, helping to bind the units of society together, whether tribes, nations or superstates. But they are essentially static, not creative. Bergson explains this in terms of 'morality', which, he says, 'comprises two different parts ... In the former, obligation stands for the pressure exerted by the elements of society on one another, in order to maintain the shape of the whole ... In the second there is still obligation, if you will, but that obligation is the force of an aspiration or an impetus ... Between the first morality and the second lies the whole distance between repose and movement.'[2]

After a static period in a society or civilisation, another generation may take up the torch of moral and spiritual progress, initiating a new phase of culture, or perhaps a new type of civilisation altogether. But the period following the death or retirement of the initiator of a movement or creative group is always critical.

At least in their early stages, movements such as that of St.

Francis of Assisi, reach out to change the world. He and the first friars travelled afar in this work. When a Cardinal tried to persuade him not to go abroad on a mission and rebuked him for encouraging his brethren to do the same, Francis said 'Do you think, my lord, that the Lord has sent the brethren only for these provinces? I tell you in truth that God has chosen the brethren for the profit and salvation of the souls of all mankind.'[3] Francis himself was prevented from reaching Palestine in 1214 by shipwreck, and from the Moors in Spain by illness, but succeeded in reaching Egypt in 1219 when he preached before the Sultan, afterwards continuing to Palestine. 'On his return in the early summer of 1220 he found a vast increase in the number of the friars, and in their missions, accompanied by corresponding friction between the two sections into which the movement was already dividing'. Those whom Francis had left in charge had taken action contravening his ideals, and he also found that a house had been built for the brethren, whom he ordered to leave. 'Whether because he felt unequal to the control of so vast an organization, or because of weariness of spirit due to growing laxity ... Francis resigned ... [Two years later] 'We must begin again,' he murmured, as he lay stricken with mortal sickness, 'to create a new family who will not forget humility, who will go and serve lepers, and, as in the old times, put themselves always, not merely in words but in reality, below all men.'"[4]

With the death of Francis the long conflict between moderates and zealots, who became known as 'the spiritual Franciscans', broke out into a blaze. 'The quarrel was this: Should the friars descend from the ideals of their founder to the common dreams of common day? Pope Nicholas II issued a bull which enabled the friars to have all the benefits of property, while keeping the new Rule ... [But] the consciences of the spiritual Franciscans were not satisfied. Poverty, they claimed, as Wyclif claimed in the next generation, was an indispensable note of the true Church.'[5] Some retired to remote hermitages, occasionally 'emerging to preach in the Umbrian cities, and constantly visited by the more fervent members of the Spiritual party.' Some, and their followers, were brutally persecuted when Franciscans of the mitigated Rule, backed by the papacy, declared them to be heretics. But by the middle of the next (14th) century, the Reform of the Strict Observance became possible, restoring 'something of the glory of primitive times. Combining the contemplative life of the hermitages with the missionary activities proper to the friars, the Strict Observance provided a frame within which some of the spirit of Franciscan mysticism could survive, and gradually absorbed into its ranks all that was best in the Order.'[6]

This pattern of decline and division, followed by re-constitution, though not on the original creative level, tends to be replicated in similar movements. In the case of the Franciscans, besides the formal re-constitution of the Order, there were three other significant developments. One was the development of the Third Order or Tertiaries, 'devout lay-folk bound to an austere rule of life ... a loosely-knit religious society, usually in close touch with those friars of the Spiritual Party who were struggling in the teeth of official discouragement to maintain the Primitive Rule.'[7] Second was the leading part played by women in the movement ever since Francis accepted to receive Clare, tonsuring her and her sister, and giving them the old chapel of St. Damian (which he had restored with his own hands) as the centre of a convent where the original Rule was followed, at least as long as St.Clare lived. She was followed by a remarkable array of teachers and saints: Angela of Foligno, 'whom her admirers did not hesitate to call a Mistress of Theologians';[8] St.Gertude and her sister St.Mechtilde, with St. Hildegarde, in Saxony; Margaret and Christina Ebner and others in Switzerland and western Germany; Italy (St.Catherine of Siena), England (Mother Julian of Norwich), to mention a few. Third, the trend in the movement under St.Bonaventure towards study and eminence in learning, which, he said, should not be a matter for surprise, since 'it was like the beginning and perfecting of the Church, which first began with simple fishermen and went on to include the most distinguished doctors.'[9].

In the case of the Quakers, external pressure played a part in reducing the dynamism of the Society, but many other factors also operated to this end.

In its early springtime the Quaker movement was a fine example of 'divine democracy ... a miniature Kingdom of God', as Dr.R.M.Jones calls it.[10] 'It was in conception a living organism rather than an organisation ... In theory the Society had no visible head. Nobody managed it, nobody directed it. Every step was taken, however momentous, however trivial, by the entire group acting, as it believed, under the direction and guidance of the Spirit.'

But like other prototype societies, the time came when the Quakers ceased to be dynamic. Instead of changing people and conditions, they drifted into a state of eminent respectability. The dead hand of custom, routine, ritual, habit, in a word 'law' took the place of 'spirit' as the guiding factor. Organisation began to be important. 'To organise is to come under the sway of habit and custom,' Dr.Jones remarks. 'It more or less locks up a movement and turns it into a system.' George Fox himself did much to build up an organisation for the Society, in order to have questions of finance and discipline adequately looked after. But before long the monthly and quarterly meetings were issuing codes which regulated the tiniest minutiae of dress and behaviour.

The return to formalism and convention was due to a change of direction on the part of the general body of Quakers, which occurred without most members being conscious of it. During the period of persecutions they longed for freedom to follow their religious practices without constant interruption. Their leaders increasingly devoted their efforts to arrange matters with the authorities by diplomatic means. In this they had considerable success, especially through William Penn, who was by birth a member of the governing class, in his dealings with James II. Fox, in the earlier period, had indeed notable conversations with Oliver Cromwell as head of State – but with the object of 'gathering' him into the new society. Now the Society set itself to become ultra-respectable to avoid shocking the susceptibilities of the world.

Enforcing conformity was also a response to the divisions which at one time were threatening to sunder the Society into a number of splinter sects. 'In checking aberrations from the standard conduct [the Society] limited the large guidance which had been the glory of the first Quaker adventure, to guidance within a confined area of action.'[11] Younger men and women or new adherents found a lack of the earlier sense of adventure and limitless possibilities. There was less of that dangerous and outgoing living which had thrown the pioneers continually on God for help and enlarged their spiritual powers.

While the emphasis on conformity in externals increased, the preoccupation of Quakers with their inward quality of life correspondingly diminished. With the second and third generation of Quakers it became progressively more difficult to resist the drift towards conformity, because in addition to those who had become Quakers by 'convincement' there were those who had been born into the Quaker fold and who had accepted their parents' conviction at second-hand.

The Quakers ceased to demand of one another that high standard of inner spiritual vitality which had been the prize of the pioneers; they took for granted both themselves and those who lived up to an external standard as doing all that was necessary. This 'maintenance of an [external] standard, itself an essentially 'static' conception, became the main object of the Society.'[12] And as in the case of the monastic movement of previous centuries, the growing wealth of the Quakers as a body had an adverse effect on their spiritual quality. The sobriety, thrift and industry of the Quakers, together with their honesty and reputation for plain dealing led often to their worldly prosperity, and since they spent little on themselves their money tended to accumulate. Many who as young men without wealth or position were spiritually aflame, became later materially minded and spiritually dead – but they continued to be regarded as members of the

Quaker community, often even as its pillars.

Finally there was a failure in the realm of thought. The pioneers like Fox had a rich background of ideas derived from intense study of the Bible and other religious literature, and from constant touch with Christians of various creeds and sects. To this body of ideas, their inheritance from the vast treasury of Christian experience which had been accumulated down the ages, they related their fresh, new experience of the indwelling Spirit of Christ — and these ideas they modified or developed in the light of this first-hand experience. But those who came after tended to accept both the ideas and the experience at second-hand. There failed to appear from among the Quakers those who combined, like St.Paul, the ability both to interpret and inspire — to express their message in terms which were valid for that world. But new life came in, during the 18th century, when Quakers raised the issue of abolishing slavery, the first great public issue (apart from religion) affecting intimately the culture of the nation, and indeed of nations world-wide.[13]

The experience of the Wesleyans, or Methodists as they came to be called, was the more usual one of splitting up. John Wesley had arranged for the 'Legal Hundred' or Conference, composed of full-time ministers, to have authority for managing the affairs of what became a separate Church (the link with the Church of England was only cut finally four years after his death). But before long the itinerant preachers and laity requested to participate in the Conference, 'so that there might be some form of popular government in the body ... [but] this was peremptorily rejected.' Difficulties arose — the overseas work was chaotic. 'The ministers were willing to increase their own power ... but not to give power to others.' A secession immediately took place and the Methodist New Connection was established.[14]

In mainstream Methodism those who were prepared to take on administration, especially if they were good at it, acquired power and authority. Notable among these was Jabez Bunting, already qualified when quite young as a medical doctor — in all respects an excellent man, who was several times Chairman or 'Moderator' of Conference, but he could not stop the disputes. The consequent secessions took away about half of the membership by the middle of the 19th century, though the breakaway Churches did not necessarily lose their vitality and continued to contribute to the high level of Christian culture which was progressively achieved during Queen Victoria's reign.[15]

As regards Moral Re-Armament, Frank Buchman in his last months 'seems to have felt that many of his colleagues had become dependent on each other and had lost the infectious spirit that changes lives, and that this was leading, as numbers grew, to an institutionalism which he had always aimed to avoid.'[16] At Caux in 1961 Buchman gave his last challenge in his speech 'Brave Men Choose' to his team as well as to the world at large. The unease he had been feeling focused at this time on his American colleagues. 'He was in an agony of spirit at what he regarded as his failure to transmit to them the depth of his own experience. Would they be able to tackle the future without him, a situation which could not now be long delayed?'[17]

When, shortly afterwards, Buchman died, Peter Howard found himself 'in charge' of MRA. He never liked the phrase. 'So many seem to think it is a kind of grab for power. For me it means doing the simple things, like giving myself to all people all the time regardless of how I am feeling or how they are behaving ... It means the knowledge that we must somehow get the discipline of Christ's Cross back into our affairs if we are going to go forward ... I feel not one whit more 'in charge' than anyone else who will bear the brunt.'[18] But, as he said, Buchman had 'paid me the compliment ... of holding me responsible for anything that went wrong anywhere in the world concerning our work, regardless of whether I knew anything about it or not ... In this sense I felt myself 'in charge' in so far as a man ever is in charge, for a long time before Buchman died'.[19]

Howard took on the task of teamwork not only with American colleagues but with those of all nationalities. He had in fact a special concern for America, and spent most of his last months there during the four years that were left him after Buchman's death. 'His love for that country and her people had grown with the years ... He was almost un-British, not in his language or his affection for his country, but in his commitment and enthusiasm which were like a gust of fresh air. He spoke to Americans with hope: 'The hard truth is that our fate, like the fate of the rest of humanity rests in your hands. Without American blood and treasure there would be no liberty left on earth today. If America fails the world fails, but America will not fail. America morally re-armed will capture the allegiance of the entire world, Communist and non-Communist alike, and will lead man into an age of justice, sanity, freedom and lasting peace.''[20]

But he had no illusions about the difficulties. 'It seems to me that so many people will only do what they are fully convinced is bound to be a colossal and recognised success ... a determination to make the rest of the world like America, and a belief that anybody who says America needs change is anti-God ... We must deal with this colossal perversion that this attitude of protectiveness towards America represents ... I feel frankly the demoralisation of a decadent giant in some of the actions and utterances from this country, and I must say so.'[21]

'It was this sense of need,' says his daughter, 'plus his passionate, all-out fight, which enabled Howard to win young people.'[22] His 1964 campaign in American universities and colleges was an extraordinary achievement, bringing 2,400 young people to Mackinac that year, to a conference for 'Tomorrow's America', whose objective was 'to raise a force of young Americans more disciplined and revolutionary, and more dedicated to building a world that works than any Communist, Fascist or other materialist.'

'Howard warned those who lived in the MRA conference centre that there would be a flood of young people, but they hardly believed him. Some were horrified when the mass of youngsters, with their jazz bands, guitars and wild clothes began to arrive on the island.'[23]

A sample of his words at the conference is as follows: 'Last night we rejoiced in the talent, fun and magic of youth .. But with all the force at my command, I tell you, it will take more than music and laughter to carry us through the crisis that confronts America. You have to save a corrupt society from self-destruction, and to bring sanity back to a civilisation that is becoming a moral and spiritual nut-house. And time is running out.'[24]

Howard returned to America and Canada in late autumn, travelling constantly, speaking wherever he went. He was frequently exhausted, but fatigue did not deter him. During his visit to America in 1962 he had already had an experience which might have been serious. 'As the final speaker after the play [in the Biltmore Bowl Theatre at Los Angeles] I suddenly found my knees wilting and my feet buckling. I nearly fell over. It was just tiredness I think.' In 1964 during one ten-week visit in America he made 46 speeches in 25 cities, followed by longer visits and more intensive speaking. 'There is a crushing programme arranged for me,' he wrote on 14th November 1964, 'but I will do it gladly. Our hour has come in this country and the world, and we must claim the faith and strength to meet it.' At one of the meetings on this programme, at Dartmouth, 'the great hall was packed – about 1,100. Everything went with swinging power, though I was dead weary.' After the night following the meeting he was besieged by questioners, and again from 6 o'clock next morning until he had to 'dash away' to catch his plane. His comment was 'we need to plan for the rebirth of humanity'.[25]

A fortnight later he was saying 'we have the answer to the splintering and chaos that is pressing on, and I want to reach as many as I can, as swiftly as I can, and while there is still time to do it. But there are so many things to do and so few folk with the bite and muscle of the heart and will that compel relentlessness ... I am weary but not woeful.' He went home briefly at the end of

137

this programme, his daughter continues, 'but returned to spend Christmas in America. On January 8th, 1965, he left the United States and returned to London ... He was to spend barely four days in London, during which time he saw all his children, his two grandchildren, and visited his farm.' His wife was on her way to Latin America where Howard was to join her within a week.

After a state reception on 15 January at Rio de Janeiro airport, with 'a vast crowd' behind the welcoming committee, and several days of enthusiastic meetings in Brazil, he flew on with his wife and accompanying party to the Argentine, Uruguay and Chile. In each country he met the Presidents and conferred with their other leaders. 'On February 21st he landed at Lima, Peru. [He] was weary, but in high spirits. He gave a press conference on arrival, and attended a party at a friend's house ... Late that night, after returning from the party, Howard was shaken by a severe fever ... On February 23rd he was taken into hospital with virus pneumonia. He was fearfully weak ... It was hard for a man who had overcome so many obstacles in life to conceive that he had met one he would not overcome in this world ... He was well cared for, but the virus was not checked and at 1 p.m. on February 25th, 1965, he died.' He was only 57.[26]

Peter Howard was a phenomenon, one of those remarkable figures who appear at times of crisis to change the course of history. Buchman was another. They can be compared with the prophets of old, or with men like Augustine, Benedict or Gregory, or a statesman like Constantine I, who salvaged what was best in the decaying culture of Antiquity, setting new trends and norms which led to the burgeoning of new civilisations. Howard was a many-sided, highly creative genius, sportsman, author, playwright, poet, farmer, whose dynamism and warmth made friends wherever he went, despite his powerful challenges which could lead to opposition when they failed to bring people to the Cross.

Howard's impact on personalities and the public had been not only through his speeches, and talks with groups and individuals, but also through his books and plays. Just before his death, in the ambulance which was taking him to hospital, despite his extreme weakness he dictated the outline for the final act of the play he had been writing in the early mornings ('Happy Deathday').

His last show to be performed in his life-time, 'Space is so startling', inspired a group of young Americans to produce another called 'Sing-Out'. Its theme song 'Up with people', along with its other songs and sketches, was a great success. 'It was undoubtedly a superb show ... 200 young men and women, singing and dancing to inspired music and lyrics ... But the moral and spiritual content of the original production had been superseded by a more specifically patriotic and educational theme. The success of the show itself seemed to be the chief objective.'[27]The medium was becoming more important than the message.

'After many years of not infrequent attacks and misinformation about MRA, suddenly there was spectacular success and popularity for this show.'[28] Desire for success together with respectability encouraged a move towards less demanding standards than Buchman's. 'Many older colleagues of Buchman and Howard..feared that some of MRA's most basic and universal foundations were being eroded.'[29] Nevertheless a secession began: those wanting to go along with 'Sing-Out' separating themselves from the mainstream committed to Buchman's way. In 1968 'Sing-Out' changed its name to 'Up With People' and incorporated itself separately, selling valuable offices and centres which had earlier been donated to Buchman for his work. Mainstream MRA practically disappeared from the United States for a time.

Howard's death removed perhaps the only man whose impact on the youth of the country might have reversed the trend towards the USA becoming, in his own words, 'a decadent giant', sinking into the non-caring 'culture of contentment'. 'Sing-Out' had a similar effect in Germany, though MRA continued as before in Britain, France, Switzerland, India and elsewhere.

The split which Howard had foreseen as possible had occurred. The circumstances in which this happened were also those which, he had said, were likely to bring on such a result. Some years before, in 1950, Howard had written: 'I have been thinking a lot about youth. My heart is very much with them. I feel that many of them, if not most, have never known the deeper experience of the Cross where their self-will is handed over. What you get is a steely philosophy, garlanded and rendered charming by the attraction of youth which has made up its mind to have its own way on many points and yells 'dictatorship' if anybody tries to stop it. Adults must not be allowed to stifle, smother or stereotype youth. Equally we must change this spirit in some of the young who think it is rendering the world a pioneering service by rebellion and brashness.' [30]

A little later he quoted Buchman to the same effect. 'Buchman feels that some young people have come to think they are the whole business, that they know all the answers, and that their job is to help us by rebelling against the authority of the senior people as publicly and frequently as possible. To one centre he sent the following cable yesterday, 'Youth is not the whole thing. If they won't work like everyone else, send them home. With my best compliments, Frank.''

From Rome (1950) Howard also wrote: 'Thinking of the future I know that an experience of the Cross is the only cement of our work. Any splits in our own or any other work have come through a refusal to face it. It ends fear and favour ... One thing very clear to me is that if we are not winning men to the deepest experience we are not living an ideology. It does not mean you can take everyone there all at once, but that some get there with you all the time.'[31]

Howard had this to say about his use of the word 'ideology'. 'Some think of [MRA] ideology as kindness, what we know as brotherhood, a few corners knocked off here and there and that is it. It needs more than that ... There can be a selfishness in being preoccupied with personal sin. It is nothing to do with [our] ideology unless it is related to changing people. Some people recoil from the highest challenge. They will be there always, demanding human fellowship at a low level. This has dragged most great religions down to ineffectiveness, and it is moral compromise which lies at the back of it.'[32] Nor could organisation and good works meet 'the challenge of the century ... We are in the midst of a struggle without scruple for the soul and character of the world.'[33]

1.T.S.Eliot: *Murder in the Cathedral,* in *The Complete Poems and Plays* (London 1975),244.
2.Bergson, op.cit., 42,45.
3.Paul Sabatier: *Vie de S. Françoise d'Assise* (Paris 1894),*238; Cambridge Medieval History,*VI,730-1.
4.H.B.Workman: *The evolution of the Monastic Ideal* (London 1913),290-1. The Sultan's polite reception of Francis in Egypt, after he had been captured, and the ability of the two men to communicate together, demonstrated a far better way of managing affairs than that of the Crusaders with their low morals, fanaticism and rapacious violence - of which Francis had visual evidence when present at the Crusaders' seizure of Damietta soon afterwards.
5.Ibid.,289-291,304-5.
6.*Cambridge Medieval History* (Cambridge 1932),VII,794-5.
7.*Cambridge Medieval History,*VII, 795.
8.Idem.
9.St.Bonaventure: *Epistola de tribus questionibus,*n.13;t. VIII,p.336 (trans.Michael Hutchinson) in Etienne Gilson: *La Philosophie de Saint Bonaventure* (Paris 1943).
10.W.C.Braithwaite: *The Second Period of Quakerism* (Cambridge 1961),Introduction,xxix.
11.Ibid.,537.
12.W.C.Braithwaite: *The Beginnings of Quakerism* (Cambridge 1955),521.

13.The anti-slavery movement began in Barbados, when George Fox, speaking publicly, advised slave-holders to free their slaves. When William Penn finally returned from America he freed his slaves. In mid-18th century, John Woolman and Anthony Benezet aroused public opinion about the iniquities of the slave trade, especially in Pennsylvania, which became the first state to abolish slavery. C.M.MacInnes: *England and Slavery* (Bristol 1934),141-2.
14.H.K.Skeats: *A History of the Free Churches of England* (London 1868),544-7,621-2.
15.J.H.Riff: *Jabez Bunting* (London ?1906).
16.Lean, op.cit,511*ff*.
17.Ibid.,526.
18.Anne Wolrige-Gordon: *Peter Howard: Life and Letters* (London 1969),293-4.
19.Ibid.,285.
20.Ibid.,360.
21.Ibid.,364.
22.Ibid.,366.
23.Ibid.,371.
24.Idem.
25.Ibid.,237,309,360,379.
26.Ibid.,383*ff*.
27.Clara Jaeger: *Never to lose my Vision* (London 1995),139.
28.Idem.
29.Idem.
30.Wolrige-Gordon,222.
31.Ibid.,221.
32.Ibid.,222,274.
33.Ibid.,276

IV: LOOKING TO THE FUTURE

CHAPTER 12

PREPARING TO ACT IN THE
NEW DIMENSION

Action in 'the spiritual dimension of statecraft' can be effective
and even produce 'miracles' according to Lord Soames' designa-
tion. For this to happen preparation is necessary, and for an elite
task-force such as undertook the rebuilding of French-German
relations postwar, it has to be rigorous. In that instance the
preparation of about a hundred men and women – the 'international team' – took place for three months at Lake Tahoe, moving
eventually, with further training at Mackinac, to Europe and Caux
for the key meetings of French and Germans.

Writing to his mother from Lake Tahoe, Alan Thornhill[1]
compared it to Galilee, which he knew from his months in
Palestine some time before. 'This has been a real Galilee for us all
in other ways – a time of accepting Christ again as the one and
only security in life and the one hope of ever accomplishing
anything. Some here have had transforming experiences of Christ's
power, including some of the oldest and most faithful 'leaders' of
the work. We have had long times of prayer together and lots of
personal sharing in twos and in larger groups. Terrible realisation
of our sin and failure, as individuals and as a team have come to
all of us. I have been seeing that in literal fact I am just full of
sin, that *nothing* in me, apart from Christ is any good, and that I
must repent not merely of the things I'm ashamed of, but also of
the apparently good things I'm proud of – gentlemanly instincts,
friendliness, sensitiveness, powers of speech – all these, apart
from Christ – and I have so often used them apart from Him –
are my worst sins because I make them a substitute for Him. I
realise I am not just 'a good man gone wrong', but just a 'pig in
a sty' – selfish and unclean through and through. Then comes the
wonderful old assurance that Christ loves pigs like me ...

'But this daily killing of self is a terrific business. Sometimes
it's seemed here that Christ just *couldn't* get through the colossal

145

hard pride and dishonesty in all of us. We'd share and share, challenge and challenge, and only feel more full of self and more bound by sin than ever. I know how Frank has had real agony these days in the fight to break down the hard walls of self we've built around us. Yet through it all there has been a constant promise that this will mean Pentecost for us all ... This is God's gift to us here in Tahoe to give us the power and the unity that can never be overthrown.

'I have been reading some great bits in Thomas à Kempis' Imitation of Christ. He says in one place that all life is a Cross. You can't avoid pain and suffering. If you don't accept it gladly or willingly, you have to accept it against your will. But 'bear the Cross gladly and willingly and it will bear thee. Take it grudgingly and it will be a burden to thee. Cast it from thee and there will be another heavier Cross which thou must bear.' We did not realise that suffering is of the essence of life. There is no real life without suffering. Without the capacity to suffer, you are dead. But once I accept that gladly, and accept suffering for myself and others as our chance to live, and to experience the Cross and Resurrection, then suffering is nothing to be feared. It's Christ's front door into our hearts.

'By facing suffering gladly, England is coming to life again. But here in America, the philosophy is still the other way. 'Avoid suffering at all cost. Keep out of trouble. Protect yourself. Realise your right to freedom, happiness, etc.' It's taught in every school, proclaimed from every platform. And that's the thing that *must* change, or America will have to learn like the rest of the world by disaster and destruction.

'The value of this time is being greatly increased by all the practical lessons we are learning in living together. Frank is amazing in this way. He inspects every menu and criticises it ruthlessly from the point of view of health and economy. Each meal must be a work of art, prepared with all the love and care of Christ Himself. We learn a lot about how to buy ... Frank uses it all as a working demonstration how to do business in a life-changing way ...

'We all work hard at our different camp duties. My job yesterday was the washing room and lavatories — a far cry from High Table at Hertford, but real fun in a family like this.'[2]

There evidently was fun at Tahoe besides the satisfaction of doing even the most menial jobs well, especially the creativity and liveliness of the evening 'floor-shows'. As regards the soul-searching occasions, in Alan Thornhill's letter there are many echoes of Thomas à Kempis besides the quotation. The aim in the *Imitation* is to encourage complete selflessness and so open the way fully for God's grace and guidance. 'The perfect victory,' he says 'is to triumph over ourselves. For he that keepeth himself subject, in such sort that his sensual affections be obedient to reason, and his reason in all things obedient to God, that person is truly conqueror of himself and lord of the world'[3] — a person who is (as some have shown themselves to be) the best equipped to heal the hurts and hates of individuals and nations. And in undertaking spiritual exercises towards this end — 'a laborious conflict'[4] — it is best not to 'lay thy heart open to every one, but to treat of thy affairs with the wise and such as fear God,'[5] while 'shrinking from all self-esteem'[6] by 'believing there is much more good in others'[7]than in oneself. In fact (as Thornhill quotes in similar words), 'Take not pleasure in thy natural gifts or wit, lest thereby thou displease God'.[8]

Treating of one's affairs 'with the wise and such as fear God' takes one back to St.Benedict and his Rule. As well as a daily discipline even more exacting than that of Tahoe, Benedict laid it down that 'the enlargement of the heart and the unspeakable sweetness of love' could only be achieved by rising through six degrees of humility until the seventh, when one would 'believe in one's inmost heart to be lower and viler than all'. To reach this stage one would have to confess to the Abbot 'all evil thoughts and secret sins'.[9]

The Tahoe gathering also had something in common with the Chapters-General of the Franciscans while St. Francis was still with his brethren, returning from their missions to prepare themselves for their next enterprises. It was even more like the gathering, in the early years of his mission (1210-11) at Rivo-Torto near Assisi, where natural grottoes or caves were used as temporary hermitages around a derelict leper house which served for meetings. In their individual retreats each friar was able during several successive days 'to be attentive only to the inner voice.'[10] At all stages the life of the friars differed from that of Thomas à Kempis, whose whole life (and that of most of his colleagues) was spent, after initiation, within the walls of a monastery. In contrast the friars made regular sorties to preach at Assisi or the surrounding villages. Following St. Francis, they never 'separated the contemplative from the active life'.[11] Francis himself, far from forgetting his mission, 'intervened in the political and social affairs of his country ... with faith that moves mountains.'[12]

Another instance of spiritual preparation for an action that began to change international relations in Europe and the world will one day be revealed when documents become available in the Vatican Library — the visit of John Paul II to Warsaw and the vast attendance at the public Mass there in 1979 during the still existing Communist regime — inspiring the Solidarity movement and giving new hope for freedom there and to the surrounding countries.

If spiritual force is to be deployed in Bosnia, for instance, preparation would be needed in the style of these historical precedents. In 1940 the three months training at Tahoe bore fruit at the Caux conferences six years later and subsequently. Spiritual power also contributed, perhaps decisively, to the ending of the Rhodesian civil war, with knock-on effects in Namibia and South Africa. In the case of Rhodesia/Zimbabwe the suggestion was made (see p.57) that the work of the three main bodies deploying spiritual force, the Catholic Church, the Quakers and MRA, could have been heightened by more cooperation. It follows that in a situation like Bosnia much might depend on the degree of cooperation between Churches and NGOs such as MRA and the German-based Offensive Junger Christen.

There is also personal training and preparation. Nothing was more drastic than the training that Peter Howard received from Buchman. Howard was one of the most successful younger journalists in Fleet Street when he changed from being an atheist to a deeply committed Christian. He had been forced to leave his job on the 'Daily Express' when he wrote a book about MRA, *Innocent Men*, after the editor refused to print an article he had written on that subject. Buchman was in America at the time; they met there as the war was ending. For five years the two men worked closely together, until, as Howard relates, 'from one day to the next Buchman bolted and barred every door and window in our relationship ... Once at a meal to which many important guests were invited, I was asked to sit at Buchman's table. When Buchman arrived and saw me there he at once and in a loud voice said 'take him away. I will not sit down at table with him. I do not want him among these people'. This incident was typical of our relationship at that time, and things continued so for nearly four years.'[13]

'They were, for Howard, active years, but years in the wilderness,' writes his biographer (his daughter Anne Wolrige Gordon). He 'often passed through many moments of despair ... The apparent harshness with which Buchman dealt with Howard at this period was, in reality, a measure of his trust in him. Buchman was a genius at reading and understanding men ... He saw in Howard the possibility of great leadership, coupled with weaknesses of pride, conceit and a dependence upon man's approval ... Those who knew Peter Howard in the last years of his life will understand that these four bleak years with Buchman made the achievements of the future possible.'[14]

In February 1950 Buchman invited Howard to join him in

Rome, and from then on until Buchman's death Howard worked closely with him. He wrote to his wife from Rome that the time there had 'meant for me something like the experience Buchman had in the Lake District. And while it has not given me his qualities, it has given me his level of commitment. Hold me to that.' [15]

Peter Howard could be as tough with colleagues as Buchman had been with him or with the team at Tahoe. Alan Thornhill tells of his experience.

'I had shared a room in Rome with Peter during a long period when Frank Buchman appeared to be going out of his way to criticize and oppose him ... I watched the struggle of a big man to carry the Cross, even if there were never again to be a grain of recognition, one promise of reward, one warm spark of human response, from the man whom he admired more than any other.

'Little had I realised back in Rome that Frank Buchman's drastic tackling of Peter was to be in some measure a foreshadowing of Peter's treatment of me. [Some time later] seldom a week went by without my being 'salted with the fire of discipline', as Frank sometimes described it. It might be a direct assault in private or in public. What he was getting at, I realize now, was the caution, the innate love of comfort and approval, the amateurism of the don, the soft underbelly of casual mediocrity in a world of harsh professionalism. Peter, in leadership, ... sword in hand sought out dragons of callous complacency, small thinking and easy living.

'Sometimes I felt he overstepped the mark. Once in Caux, before a group of some hundreds, he threw out a caustic comment on my character which seemed so untrue as to be intolerable. A steely resentment entered my being. Without a word to anybody I packed my things, left by a side-door, walked furiously down the steepest mountain track to Montreux and caught the train to Paris. All the way ... my heart was numb, unfeeling, possessed with only one thought, to get out and stay out for ever.

'This was the unlikely prelude to the most uncomfortable and perhaps the most stupendous night of my life. The setting was far from spiritual or inspiring. It was a sleazy Paris hotel close to the Gare de Lyon. There I lay, tossing and turning, full of rebellion and bitterness. Lovingly, gently, through a long night, Christ led me, protesting, squirming, back to the *Via Dolorosa*, and the way of the Cross ... What was my wounded pride compared to that blood and sweat, the hammer of the nails, the taunts of the crowd? Beyond that, what of my own hatred and betrayal? That night fear left me. I was no longer a slave to what other people said or thought. On my knees beside that lumpy bed, I was emptied of self, alone with God. I was my own man. Let others say what they will, do what they will. 'What is that to thee? Follow thou Me'.

'And then a further gift. As the wintry light of morning crept into the room, I realized something else. I cared for Peter. He was not my enemy. He was my friend who had helped to drive me towards the Cross of Christ, the most precious gift in my life. I found in my heart a longing, an eagerness to see him again. For the first time I might be able to talk with him as man to man ... [Eventually] we had searching, caring talk between equals, equal in responsibility, equal in need. It was the kind of fearless honesty he must have longed for so much and experienced so seldom. At the end he made an unexpected request. He asked me to travel with him and be his chaplain.'[16]

This experience and the earlier experience at Tahoe were the kind that could form men and women into movers of mountains – of hatred, rapacity, lust and fear, forging new links between nations and ethnicities, creating a culture of caring in place of the prevailing culture of contentment among the well-to-do. It might, in Christian terms, be an experience of the Cross such as Buchman's, a calling such as Alec Smith's, or a time in the wilderness such as that of Peter Howard. Anyone aiming at effective action in the spiritual dimension of statecraft should welcome and cherish such experiences.

While Buchman made no secret of his experience of the Cross

as 'an aweful and devastating contact with the holiness of God,[17] which breaks but remakes, which condemns but cures', he could also present it in quite un-theological terms, making it accessible to those who were not Christians or indeed of no religion at all. At the end of a meeting at Caux in 1948 he said: 'What was dominant in my mind was, "A mighty movement of God's living Spirit throughout the lands. A movement where everyone has a part because this is a work for everyone, everywhere." Fifteen minutes in the morning, listen ten and talk five. Try it. God is there. We are here and the other person is there. God speaks to us and God speaks to the other person. There is only one thing that can stop us. It is a little word, sin. S I N. Take that middle letter "I". If you put an I on its beam end you get a minus sign. What you need to do with that I is to lengthen that line between God and the other person and you get a cross. You can do that in the morning and write it down. I found I got so many things I had to write them down because I could not remember them. Someone in China said "The strongest memory is weaker than the palest ink."'[18]

This may be the central point of the new paradigm in international relations that is being called for. Civilisation has grown by increments since mankind first turned to permanent settlements in the Nile Valley and elsewhere. Change comes through culture, not DNA, and culture, as in the matter of wearing clothes, can be passed on from generation to generation, with many elaborations. Personal and tribal disputes were originally settled by violence with primitive weapons of stone and wood. The 'art' of war has now developed into massacres and genocide with sophisticated armaments and nuclear weaponry. A cultural change as definite as the transition from nudity to clothes can alone save humanity from self-extinction. The price is the abandonment of violence in personal and political relationships, while seeking the Mind of God (or 'the Wisdom Mind')[19] in all matters great and small.

1.Alan Thornhill to his mother, 11/8/80.

2.Alan Thornhill (1906-1988) graduated in Theology at Hertford College, Oxford, was ordained and became a Curate at Peckham in South London. In 1930 he was invited by the Principal of Hertford to return as Chaplain and Fellow, proceeding in 1937 to Wycliffe Hall, Oxford, as Lecturer in Theology. In 1939 he went to America with Frank Buchman, returning to Europe with others of 'the international team' of MRA in 1946. Author of *The Forgotten Factor*.

3.Thomas à Kempis: *The Imitation of Christ*, Book III,ch.53,vs.2.

4.Ibid.,III,12,vs.5.

5.Ibid.,I,8,vs.1

5.Ibid.,III,8,vs.1.

7.Ibid.,I,7,vs.3.

8.Ibid.,I,8,vs.2.

9.D.Oswald Hunter Blair (editor): *The Rule of St.Benedict* (Fort Augustus 1906).

10.Paul Sabatier: *Vie de S.François d'Assise* (Paris 1894),124.

11.Ibid.,125.

12.Ibid.,127-8.

13.Anne Wolrige Gordon, op.cit.,204-5.

14.Idem.

15.Ibid.,221.

16.Alan Thornhill: *Best of Friends* (London 1986),196*ff.*

17.Peter Marsh and Hugh Elliott: *Hope for Today* (London 1995),72.

18.Mountain House, Caux: Archive.

19.See Appendix 3:5 (Lord Rees-Mogg).

CHAPTER 13

ACTION FOR THE COMING AGE

In addition to moral and spiritual preparation, there are four other conditions which must be observed if operating in 'the missing dimension of statecraft' is to produce the desired effects. One is knowledge about the situation, for instance ex-Yugoslavia – a necessity so obvious that it hardly needs mentioning, though it is well to bear in mind the advice of Harold Saunders to those functioning as members of NGO's: 'Citizens may be more effective if they stop to educate themselves in policy thinking ... A multitude of well-meaning citizens craving new relationships of peace and growth may waste a lot of precious energy if they fail to direct that energy precisely to the goals and objectives that need to be achieved' – while remembering that as ordinary citizens they are in a position to bring changes at the grass-roots in a way which professionals ('track one') might find difficult.[1]

Secondly there is the need to reach out to 'the other person', as Frank Buchman put it, crossing out the 'I' while extending the line of caring to someone, whether of low or high degree, the politician as well as the ordinary person. In Buchman's case it might be a Senator at Washington, whether known or not as a President in waiting, or the young man who brought him his breakfast.

Thirdly there should be continuity in this work if it is to achieve the global transformation that is urgent, each advance making possible the next, in the way that the Zimbabwe settlement made possible that of Namibia, which in turn encouraged the moves to end apartheid and bring in the new regime in South Africa.

Fourthly, there must be a readiness to apologise and forgive by at least a minority, however small, of those involved in the conflict, such as Arthur Kanodereka responding to Alec Smith's apology, so paving the way for the historic meeting of Alec's father with Robert Mugabe; of Irène Laure asking the Germans to forgive her hatred; of the Dutch Reformed Church leaders apologising publicly for misusing Scripture to support apartheid; of De Klerk's initiative and the response from Nelson Mandela and Archbishop Tutu.

How to fulfil these conditions in a situation like ex-Yugoslavia, assuming that the moral and spiritual preparation has been adequate? Knowledge of some history may be essential, bringing to mind that, since the Roman Empire, the centuries of war and changes of regime left much of the Balkans, notably Bosnia-Herzogovina, in the Dark Ages — even such progress as the Middle Ages achieved had not reached that province by the 1870s when Austria-Hungary took over its administration from Turkey. There were no towns — even Sarajevo and Mostar were not much more than large villages. Industry had not replaced peasant handicrafts; most trading was by barter. 'There were few schools and practically no medical services; plague, cholera and syphilis were rife ... The peasant scratched the ground with a wooden plough to raise a meagre crop of maize, or pastured his lean cattle, sheep and swine on the hill-tops and in the forests. There was little law and order, especially for the Christian population.'[2]

All this began to change in 1882 with the appointment of Benjamin Kallay, a Hungarian, as chief administrator. Under his 'enlightened autocracy' schools and agricultural colleges were built and staffed, 'over 1,000 miles of railways were built ... Medical and veterinary services were improved out of all recognition ... The Government devoted special pains to encouraging cottage industries ... '[3] But before Kallay's death in 1903 development was slowing down, while his mistrust of the Serb component of the population generated resentment which sparked the assassination of the Archduke Franz Ferdinand at Sarajevo in 1914. Progress was halted in the war that followed, while assassination, which had been a normal part of politics in the area, continued with the murder — this time by a Croat — of King Alexander of Yugoslavia in 1934.[4] The terrorist Pavelić, involved in that murder, was made the ruler of so-called 'independent' Croatia after the Germans overran Yugoslavia in the second World War, and with his followers of the Ustase massacred Serbs 'more ostentatiously than the Germans massacred Jews'.[5] Tito, taking over Yugoslavia as the war ended, held the disparate population in check while modernisation was resumed, only to be arrested again, after his death in 1980, with the outbreak of the war, initially between Slovenes, Croats and Serbs, in 1991.

The Muslims, mostly in Bosnia, were involved as the conflict spread. Religion is the defining element as much as (if not more than) ethnicity. Accordingly it may well be through religion, as 'the missing dimension of statecraft', that the best contribution can be made towards defusing the conflict, with the hope of eventually ending it altogether. So the attendance of the Orthodox Bishop in Bosnia and the Catholic Archbishop at the ceremony installing the present Reis-ul-elema, Dr Mustafa Ceric, is an encouraging augury, as was the call of Monsignor Mato Zovic, Vicar-General of the Catholic Archdiocese in Sarajevo, for 'the media, priests and imams, political representatives and non-governmental organisations, patiently and gradually to dismantle the hostile mentality within their own ethnic and religious communities.'[6] A further step forward was a forum at the Islamic Centre at Zagreb, called by the Mufti of Croatia and the Director of the Catholic Tecaj-Cursillo Training Centre there.

Catholics and Protestants, members of the Western Churches, may have to apologise, or at least change their mode of proceeding, in respect of typical Western pushiness and urge to dominate. The way in which the Catholic and Orthodox Churches separated did little credit to either of them, though Rome must surely bear the bulk of the blame in the bitter disputes on points of theology with the Patriarch at Constantinople, especially Photius in the 9th century, and the excommunication of Michael Cerularius by Leo IX, who sent the anathema to be laid by the papal legates on the altar of Hagia Sophia in July 1054. Apology is also due for the capture and partial wrecking of Constantinople in the Fourth Crusade, and the forced submission of the Patriarch. The possibility of sincere apologies long after the outrages occurred was demonstrated by Pope Paul VI, who visited Patriarch Athenagoras, kneeling down and kissing his feet.

Some expression of repentance and change of attitude in our Western dealings with the rest of the world is needed. Besides the Orthodox Church, this applies to relations with Islam, in which (a century before the breach between the Eastern and Western Churches) Byzantium had shown a better — and quite un-theological — way when the Caliph Al-Hakam II at Cordoba requested help from Emperor Nicephorus Phocas in decorating the mihrab in the great Mezquita Mosque (which occupied the site of a former church). 'The Emperor not only sent a specialist in mosaic work but about 16 tons of stone and glass cubes with which he was to work.'[7] This recess, with its glory of colour and intricate patterns, facing towards Mecca — an essential element in the architecture — is still in place.

Action in 'the missing dimension' directed to particular areas or issues is most effective if it is part of a *general* action to deal with the basic ills which are threatening civilised living in a viable habitat. While evil works to aggravate and exploit all natural tendencies to decline and dissolution, there is a creative element in the universe which constantly brings into being new material structures and (in our planet) new forms of life through processes of spontaneous organisation — and the nearer chaos looms the more these processes are stimulated. 'At the edge of chaos' situations develop which are 'highly sensitized to change', to borrow the language of those pioneers of science who continue to discover new secrets about our amazing habitat.[8] And the 'edge of chaos' can equally apply to the condition we have reached in the world today, if we accept the thesis expounded by Gleick, that in 'the boundary region between order and chaos' regularities are usually found which involve 'a completely different kind of behaviour'. Through such 'phase transitions' evolution takes place.[9] Some species, including our own, when faced by climatic changes or other hazards, have successfully adapted by way of such transitions, while some have become extinct.

Professor Stuart Kauffman, who is in the van of this pioneering, explains that his aim in developing the 'spontaneous organization' theory is 'not so much to challenge as to broaden the neo-Darwinian tradition'[10] that ascribes all evolution in the realm of biology to natural selection — the survival of the fittest. However un-trained we may be in science generally and this branch of science in particular, we may find that this research into the origins and development of life presents a new vision of the possible future for mankind. While disclaiming belief in divine intervention, Kauffman, 'in the language of mathematics, logic, and science [expresses] a kind of primal mysticism ... Darwin didn't know about self-organization — matter's incessant attempts to organize itself into ever more complex structures, even in the face of the incessant forces of dissolution described by the second law of thermodynamics. Nor did Darwin know that the forces of order and self-organization apply to the creation of living systems just as surely as they do to the formation of snowflakes or the appearance of convection cells in a simmering pot of soup. So the story of life is, indeed, the story of accident and happenstance ... but it is also the story of order: a kind of deep, inner creativity that is woven into the very fabric of nature.'[11]

This points to 'a world philosophy capable of creating a new era of constructive relationships between men and nations',[12] based on the recognition that the Power which constantly creates and recreates, at the edge of a chaos towards which all things tend, 'is not the product of blind chance, but is controlled by purpose.'[13] These words of the philosopher B.H.Streeter, are amply corroborated by the latest discoveries of science. Life can only exist by means of 'myriads of proteins and sugars and lipids and nucleic acids that you need to make a fully functioning cell ... Even to produce *one* useful protein molecule, if the formation were truly random, you would have to wait for longer than the lifetime of the Universe'. But (quoting Stuart Kauffman again) 'life had not been just a random accident, but was part of nature's incessant compulsion for self-organisation.'[14] This dynamic of continuous creation suggests that there is design in the Universe. Design implies purpose, and since purpose is the function of will and will implies personality, we can envisage this personality as a Being whom, in our Abrahamic faiths, we call God.

For us humans it follows that to be in touch with Him or 'the Wisdom Mind'[15] must be our aim in life. Our own purposes and plans can only work, at least in the longer term, if they are part of the wider purposes of God. He must have a decisive place in our lives. 'It is a contradiction in terms,' continues Streeter, 'to say that God exists but has no plan. And to say that His plan can only contemplate the big outline and not also the minor detail, is to reduce his intelligence to the scale of ours. The Divine Intelligence cannot be content with something less full of purpose and precision than what a human general or statesman would call a 'plan''.[16] He works through us with a strategy for the future of Mankind which we can glimpse in vision — the vision which gives passion and determination so to change and discipline ourselves that we become part of His creative minority for remaking the world.

The concept of 'the creative minority' is one of A.J. Toynbee's seminal phrases. Toynbee sees the first creative minority in history as that which effected the 'miraculous act' of the transition from primitive tribalism to the first civilisations. Subsequently creative minorities have been 'the leaders of any given civilisation at any given stage in the history of its growth.'. Defining a creative minority's mission, he says it 'is to perform its work of creation, not just for itself, but for the benefit of the whole of society to which it belongs.[17]

Kauffman worked out many of his ideas at the Santa Fe Institute, New Mexico, where scientists of every variety mingle

159

with economists, historians, social scientists, all working together in matters concerned with the 'sustainability' of the planet. For example, an economist heard Kauffman expound another of his ideas, that 'cells in embryos send out chemical messengers to trigger the development of other cells in the embryo in a self-consistent network' — which immediately 'resonated with his ideas on the self-consistent, mutually supportive webs of interactions in human societies.'[18] One does not have to be an economist to realise that such insights can underline the importance of strengthening this kind of social bonding while enhancing the vision of those involved. The resulting action can be a contribution to 'sustainability'.

The Nobel Prize-winning physicist Murray Gell-Mann helped to set up the World Resources Institute at Washington, where 'at least six fundamental transitions within a very few decades' have been defined as essential if global sustainability is to be assured, starting with a demographic transition to a roughly stable world population. Other 'transitions' concern safeguarding the environment while technology develops, setting economic standards so that the world lives off nature's 'income' rather than depleting its 'capital', and ensuring 'a broader sharing of that income'. With all this it will be necessary to 'facilitate a global attack on global problems,' and to use the opportunities of the information transition to enable 'large numbers of people to understand the nature of the challenges they face.' To get from here to there will require, says Gell-Mann, 'the renunciation or sublimation or transformation of our traditional appetites: to outbreed, out-consume, and conquer our rivals ... These impulses may once have been adaptive. Indeed, they may even be hard-wired into our brains. But we no longer have the luxury of tolerating them.'[19]

A scientist of the previous generation, Pierre Lecomte du Noüy, assserted that 'only evolution could bring forth Man ... The intervention of an Idea, a Will, a supreme intelligence, throws a little light on the combined transformation leading through an uninterrupted line to Man. In Man ... alone, the possibility of choice has been transformed into a moral idea: in order to evolve *he must no longer obey Nature.* He must criticize and control his desires which were previously the only Law. We are still at the dawn of human evolution ... Many important steps in evolution started out as a mutation affecting only a very small number of individuals, perhaps only one – certain rare, privileged men, comparable to the transitional animals who were in advance of their time. These men attained a higher stage of evolution ... When the human body reached a state of relative perfection ... evolution had to continue on another plane ... the spiritual plane.'[20]

There have to be strategies that will work best in 'an infinite space of possibilities.'[21] It is here that Buchman's 'laboratory time' at Pennsylvania State College is relevant. In his own change and in bringing change to others Buchman was sharing in the experience of the prophets and founders of the great faiths. The simplicity and directness of this approach cannot be overlooked. While another philosopher, Albert Schweitzer, could say that 'the only conceivable way of bringing about a reconstruction of our world on new lines is first of all to become new men ourselves,'[22] Buchman showed how this could happen because it had happened to himself, through an experience, as dramatic as that of Augustine in the garden at Milan, of reconciliation with his Maker, leading on to his regular morning times of quiet.[23]

An experimental time of quiet has marked for many people the start of a new way of life – but does this really mean a change in our nature? The usual drives and urges may still be there, but new motivations take the place of the old ones. There is new discipline in daily life. Call it the building of new *character*, but in any case the scriptural phrase is surely still admissible as used by St.Paul: 'Adapt yourselves no longer to the pattern of the present world, but let your minds be renewed and your whole nature thus transformed.'[24]

One man described his experience of change as 'a bomb

which exploded amidst everything that was wrong and defiled in myself, followed by the reconstruction of my whole personality on new foundations.'[25] Although personal change may not be so dramatic for everyone, St.Paul's emphasis on renewal of the mind is noteworthy — the dynamic of new ideas coming, as they often do, out of silence, to echo the title of Professor Theophil Spoerri's book.[26] It is an ideology of world change through personal change, based on God having the direction of our lives, a change which enables us to have a positive part in the change which is taking place in the whole species Mankind. Modern inventions have been changing the material basis of our living, and such changes, as Marx rightly pointed out, change the 'superstructure' too, of art, literature, law and politics — in fact the entire culture. But Hegel was also right: *ideas* are the dominant factor in determining the way these changes go. The one world of speedy travel and instant communication, along with all the other consequences of scientific and industrial change, have inevitably brought us to the new era which is opening — but ideas will determine its character and duration. It was not the beginning of modern industry in Russia that brought on Lenin's revolution — it was his ideology, derived from Marx and Engels; nor was it the economic consequences of the first World War that brought Hitler to power, but his ideology derived from Darwin's theory of the survival of the fittest. So Buchman also saw that 'the culture of contentment' — in other words materialism — was not going to bring a satisfying and harmonious way of life in America or the world as a whole.

'Moving out of our comfort zone can be the single most important step we can make towards creating peace and understanding in our hearts and in the world' is a comment from the younger generation.[27] But how, it may be asked, can our limited personalities and our relatively brief lives have the kind of effect on a world of humans which seems heading for disaster? There may indeed be disaster — at this turning-point in history humanity is on a knife-edge – we are 'at the edge of chaos': the build-up of conflicts to a nuclear catastrophe, or even the exhaustion of resources and the pollution of the planet, may mean the end of what we may regard as God's original purpose for Mankind. Yet we must not underrate the effects of even a single life wholly devoted to Him, especially at the beginning of vast changes which, whether for good or ill, are going to alter radically the mode of human living. At such a moment the smallest inputs can have enormous consequences in determining the outcome – another parallel with what happens in the physical world, a concept popularised by Edward Lorenz in the 'butterfly effect': 'a butterfly stirring the air today in Peking can transform storm systems next month in New York'.[28]

Allowing that the analogy was expressed 'half-jokingly', what for any of us, young, old, strong or feeble, might be the moral equivalent of the flap of a butterfly's wings? In a world where dishonesty, sleaze and corruption seem to be gaining ground every day, the stand taken by one individual on the standard of absolute honesty, which then encourages others, may be the start of a radical change in tackling corruption in our own community and in society generally. Similarly the standard of absolute purity brings guidelines and convictions which enable us to renounce, sublimate or transform 'our traditional appetites', to quote Gell-Mann again, although 'they may even be hard-wired into our brains.'

Such words may readily find a response from the generation brought up in the culture stemming from the traditional faiths, but what about those exposed from early years to the pill-and-condom culture of today? 'Wherewithal shall a young man keep his way pure?' asks the Psalmist[29] – and the question has to be asked of a young woman too. With television and the other media endlessly trivialising sex or putting out blatant pornography, the way for the young is difficult indeed. Even so, persons of any age can pass through periods of doubt or depression, like Dante in the dark wood, when a sense is alerted that some kind of belief or philosophy alone can deal with the feelings of inadequacy or futility. Then, at the moment of knocking on the door of truth, it opens, and the search may begin, whole-hearted in the Psalmist's words, leading to 'delight' in the path as it opens out.[30]

At that point the great truths are clarified, and marriage is seen as a 'holy estate' in which the man and the woman become 'one flesh'. These are strong words, emphasising the life-long bonding with stability for the family which may be inhibited by certain kinds of pre-marital sexual activity (to use the bland modern phrase rather than an older realistic one).[31]

'Philosophy' may sound a rather grand word to use in this context. Academic philosophy may play a part for those who are students — indeed Allan Bloom connects the whole decline of culture in the United States with the decline of philosophy as taught at universities — though much more important, in his view, has been the decline of the family from the days when 'attending church or synagogue, praying at the table, were a way of life, inseparable from the moral education that was supposed to be the family's special responsibility in this democracy. [But now] the dreariness of the family's spiritual landscape passes belief. The moral supplement' of philosophy is needed to draw strength from 'the great remains of a tradition that have grown senile.' History too is needed, for we are 'like ignorant shepherds living on a site where great civilisations once flourished. The shepherds play with the fragments that pop up to the surface, having no notion of the beautiful structures of which they were once a part ... The new language is that of *value* relativism.' [32]

It follows that unselfishness and love become meaningful as *absolute* standards for constant aspiration — and challenge — though even in a long life really loving one's neighbour as oneself is scarcely or only intermittently attained except by a dedicated few:　　　'... something given

　　　And taken, in a lifetime's death in love,

　　　Ardour and selflessness and self-surrender.' [33]

We can take courage from the Beirut hostage Brian Keenan, who on regaining freedom after many harrowing months in captivity said: 'I know now that I make history in every touch I have with people, even how I greet people in the street.' To quote B.H. Streeter again:

> History shows that in case of wars, revolutions, strikes and other major conflicts, a relatively small weight of public opinion on one side or the other, or the presence or absence of moral insight and courage in a few individuals in positions of influence, has often turned the balance between a reasonable settlement and a fight to the finish. Modern civilisation can only be saved by a moral revival. But for this it would suffice if every tenth or hundredth person were changed. For each such person raises the level of those whom he touches in the home, in business, and in public affairs.[34]

In other words the transforming effect of such creative minorities is far beyond their immediate circle − it is the creation of *a new culture*. The early Christians, along with others moved by Stoicism or the religions from the Orient, changed the whole culture of Antiquity, bringing in the era which is only now coming to an end − an era paralleled by other cultures, Chinese, Buddhist, Indian, Islamic, which developed and intermingled elsewhere. But cultures do not, like old soldiers, just fade away − they can pass on their best to succeeding generations. The high Christian culture of the West had not been entirely destroyed by two world wars. It survived among people in all classes and all walks of life, besides those leaders who saved Western Europe after 1945. If we maintain their determination, with a world-shaping vision, we may all in our different ways help to bring in the new culture that is needed for the coming millennium.

1.See p.76.

2.C.A.Macartney: *The Habsburg Empire 1790-1918* (London 1968),740.

3.Ibid.,744.

4.King Alexander Obrenovich had been murdered with his queen in June 1903.

5.Elizabeth Wiskemann: *Europe of the Dictators 1919-1945* (London 1966),177.

6.Op.cit., p.83, ref.44.

7.Alfonso Lowe: *The South of Spain* (London 1973),38.

8.Professor Paul Davies, reviewing *The Origins of Order* in 'The Guardian Weekly',23/1/93. I am indebted to the late Dr. Alwyn McKay for help in this section.

9.James Gleick: *Chaos, Making a New Science* (Sphere Books - Macdonald, London 1989),100*ff.*,170,169,235.

10.Stuart A.Kauffman: *The Origins of Order* (O.U.P. 1993),26.

11.M.Mitchell Waldrop: *Complexity* (Simon and Schuster 1992; Viking 1993),102. See also Appendix 5: Dr. Alwyn Mckay: 'The chemistry of a grand design'.

12.Buchman,op.cit.,107.

13.Burnett Hillman Streeter: *The God who Speaks* (London 1943),10.

14.Waldrop,op.cit.,122,125.

15.See Appendix 3, section 5 (Lord Rees-Mogg).

16.Streeter,op.cit.,10,11.

17.A.J.Toynbee: *A Study of History*, (op.cit.), VIII,624; IV,5; IX,364.

18.Waldrop,op.cit.,100-101.

19.Ibid.,351.

20.Lecomte du Noüy: *Human Destiny* (Eng.trans. London 1947),94,,97,109-111. See also Appendix 6.

21.Waldrop,151.

22.A.Schweitzer: *The Decay and the Restoration of Civilization* (London 1932),64,60.

23.See pp.30,116; also Appendix 2: Dr.Charis Waddy: A time of quiet.

24.Romans 12:2.

25.Fernand Maton in 'Changer',October 1979,p.3. See Appendix 6 for points from the classic on this subject, William James: *The Varieties of Religious Experience* (London 1902).

26.Theophil Spoerri: *Dynamic out of Silence* (London 1976; trans. from *Dynamik aus der Stille,* Caux Verlag, Luzern 1971).

27.'Global Express',vol.3,no.1,1977,p.5.

28.Gleick,8.

29.Psalm 119,v.9. Translation from A.Cohen: *The Psalms* (The Soncino Press, Hindhead UK 1945).

30.Dante: *Inferno,*Canto 1. Matthew 7 v.7; Luke 11 v.9. See also Appendix 6,Personal change.

31.Church of England Marriage Service; Matthew,19:4*ff.*

32.Allan Bloom: *The Closing of the American Mind (*Simon and Schuster,USA 1987 and Penguin,UK 1988), 56-7,239,141.

33.T.S.Eliot: no. v in *The Dry Salvages, Four Quartets (The Complete Poems and Plays,* London 1969, 190).

The few quotations of poetry in this book are from T.S.Eliot, whom one may claim to be the prophetic poet of our times. Starting with the spiritual barrenness of the inter-war period in *The Waste Land* he proceeds at the end of the poem(in analogy with his own breakdown and healing) to the words from an Upanishad, 'shantih shantih shantih', which he interprets as 'the Peace which passeth understanding'. He speaks of 'the awful daring of a moment's surrender / Which an age of prudence can never retract' (pp.401-2 of the above edition), and although in 'Ash Wednesday' he 'does not hope to turn again', yet he does so. The full development of this thought comes in later poems, particularly 'The Four Quartets', where his focus is the timeless moment - 'the point of intersection of the timeless with time' (p.189: 'The Dry Salvages') - 'the critical moment that is always now and here' (*Murder in the Cathedral*, p.265). It is analgous with the thought of Jesus: 'the *teshuva*, the turning-point' of his life at his baptism

by John, when time ceases to be time for him - it 'is no longer time as we know it but has acquired a quality of finality...as it is of those who afterwards answer his own call to *teshuva*, to turn back decisively and irrevocably to God.' (Vermes,op.cit.,24)
34.Quoted in Buchman,op.cit.,351.

LORD RADSTOCK AND RUSSIA

Granville Waldegrave, third Baron Radstock, was the grandson of a fighting admiral who had been ennobled during the Napoleonic wars. He grew up in Queen Victoria's England in an age when the Evangelical Movement was at its height. This powerful spiritual upsurge had penetrated all levels of society through the Wesley brothers, Wilberforce, and many other remarkable men and women, some known and most unknown.

A movement, initiated by John Nelson Darby (a barrister who became an Anglican priest, then left the Church as a fundamentalist preacher), spread through Britain and Europe to America in the 1820's and 30's. In England his followers were known as Plymouth Brethren from a group at that city of retired officers of the East India Company. Dispensing with ministry and church organisation, their Quaker-like meetings and Calvinist teaching appealed particularly to men of discipline. Officers returning from the blood and squalor of the Crimea, who were attracted by this movement, began meeting in each others' London homes and clubs for studying the Bible and sharing their spiritual experiences. Among those caught up in 'the revival of 1857' (though he later left the Plymouth Brethren) was Lord Radstock, having served in the Crimea at the end of the war.

After graduating at Oxford, Radstock took much trouble to improve his French, travelled in the United States and elsewhere, married a duke's granddaughter who was a reigning beauty, and was set for a diplomatic career. But then came a profound change in his life. It was, in the words of his biographer, an 'entire abandonment to the service of Christ, shutting him off from the natural friendships and companionships of his age.' Handing out tracts in Rotten Row or on the sea-front at Weston-super-Mare provoked aristocratic contempt, but 'the very fact of his rejection by his own class in England led eventually to the great and worldwide influence which he exercised on individuals in many lands both East and West.'

His wife, who was wholeheartedly with him, sold her jewels. The best china went, the carriage. He gave up shooting 'in order to preach the Gospel with greater freedom.' As a much-praised officer in the Volunteer (later Territorial) Army, he had raised and commanded a battalion, drilling his men in the day-time on Saturdays, and spending the evenings with his wife and friends at home, reading and discussing passages of the Bible. The Volunteer work he gave up also, to free himself for enterprises like founding a Home in London for impoverished working women, and another in Paris for English ballet-dancers.

It was an age when Britain was the dynamo of technological progress, when frontiers throughout the world were opening and political barriers falling. This generated a certain euphoria. A map drawn up in 1863, his biographer wrote, illustrated 'the extraordinary change which had in this interval of three years, passed over the world. China, hermetically closed for 2,000 years, was opened to our Ambassadors, to trade and to travel, and to missions. In Russia, 25 million serfs were liberated; American slavery was abolished; and in countless other directions, as in Austria and Italy, the fetters of centuries were snapped asunder, and the nations delivered. The secular, and even the comic press of the day, notes with astonishment the progress in human affairs of those three eventful years.'

The post-Crimea revival, from which came such stalwarts as William Booth, founder of the Salvation Army, brought together in conferences many people 'of every denomination for worship and prayer'. A leading spirit from the top echelons of the Civil Service, Arthur Blackwood, spent 'two early morning hours, whatever the stress of life, consecrated to his Bible and his God ... Country houses became in numberless instances centres of prayer and preaching.' One of these was the home of Sir Thomas Beauchamp, whose wife was Lady Radstock's sister.

Such family links formed a network of support for those who at home or overseas were dedicating themselves to throwing out the frontiers of God's kingdom. This 'mightiest work of grace which has ever rolled over the New World,' on the eve of the American Civil War, produced outstanding evangelists, one of the best-known to visit Britain being Dwight Moody. In London in 1865, 'with American directness, he urged the necessity of a daily definite business transaction with God, in the heart of the City, as definite in its aim and purpose as those undertaken with men.'

This was the spirit of Lord Radstock, who avoided discussion of doctrine with other Christians, while winning, during his seven visits to India, lifelong friends among Hindus and Muslims. In Paris he could hand out tracts to workmen in the early morning, and call on Russian grand-duchesses in the afternoon. In a day when French was the common language of cultivated Europeans, and practically the first language of many educated Russians, Radstock was at home in the cosmopolitan society of privilege, whether in France or the other capitals. His small informal meetings, when he discussed passages from the Bible and expounded his faith in salvation through the Cross, intrigued and attracted those for whom they were a novelty.

A story, which may suggest some apocryphal elements, illustrates the character of the man.

> As a young and beautiful Russian lady was reading a novel in a railway carriage on a Swiss railway, she was startled by the unceremonious action of her fellow-traveller, a grey-haired English gentleman, who, without a word of apology or introduction, snatched the novel out of her hand and flung it out of the window. She was beginning to expostulate with him when he stopped her by asking her in a voice full of deep and tender feeling, whether she ever prayed for her country ... And then, in a very loving and patient fashion, he began to tell her of how, for many years past, he had it specially borne in upon his mind that he must pray for Russia, and get other people to pray for her. 'Look here,' said he: and producing a well-thumbed

171

pocket Bible he turned the first two pages. The lady saw, to her astonishment, the pages filled with Russian signatures, many of which she recognised as those of her friends in St. Petersburg. 'Every one of them', continued the strange Englishman, 'has signed his or her name in this Bible, promising that, for the rest of their life they will every morning and evening pray for their country. Whenever I see a Russian I always ask him to make me that promise, and I beg of you to do the same.' The lady was much impressed with the sincerity and quaintness of the request, and added her name to the others ... The conversation of the old Englishman, whose heart was consumed within him by reason of his longing for the welfare of Russia, dwelt in her memory, and led to a complete change of life.

One day in Paris, continually 'waiting upon God in the minutest details for direction and guidance', he found himself in the company of 'a certain Grand Duchess.' She had been wary of meeting Radstock, but, when it happened, five hours of conversation ensued. He was invited to St. Petersburg. This was one of several invitations from people at the highest social level. In the spring of 1874, undeterred by illness (Radstock did not believe in 'human skill' for curing maladies), he set out for Russia. His health returned as the train crossed the frontier.

At St. Petersburg it was a time of intense activity, going from house to house ten or fifteen times a day. The writer Nikolai Leskov gives a picture of some of these informal but powerfully challenging events. 'There are quite a lot of people present, but the ladies are in a large majority over the gentlemen, among whom are to be seen a few military men and two generals in dress uniform ... The civil servants wear black formal suits.' Radstock opens the proceedings by kneeling down and saying a prayer in French. After giving an exposition of Genesis ch.3,verses 9 and 10, he asks some searching questions.'If at this moment the Lord were thus to challenge each one of us: where art thou? What answer would you give Him? – 'Where art thou?' – On the narrow path leading to eternal bliss, or on the broad one – to eternal damnation? 'Where art thou?' – among the wise virgins with a good supply of oil in their lamps or among the foolish ones? 'Where art thou?' – among the servants of God or of Mammon? – I implore you, look at yourselves, take thought, give a clear response to the question while you are on this earth, while there is still time.'

With no note of disapproval of the Orthodox faith of his listeners (and no intention, as Leskov confirms, of setting up a sect), Radstock challenges those who say that they have their established religion and 'attend the customary forms of worship – what else do you need? But the Lord reads men's hearts. To your way of thinking, I know, you doubtless imagine that you serve God by muttering your prayer or performing some service to your neighbour ... A fearful and wretched state of mind to be in! To whom have you given your heart – to Him or to the world?' With reference to his Genesis text he continues: 'Throw away the garment you have made, this apron of dry leaves to which you give the high-sounding name of "good works"! Simply hurry at His call, bow the knee to the One who so loved you, and say to Him: "Accept me in the number of the least of thy servants." And He will array you in a wedding garment ...' The occasion might end with the singing of a hymn accompanied by a harmonium.

Leskov explains Radstock's success in terms of the disillusionment felt by people who had 'decided that the Russian Church retained nothing more than exterior forms and that it totally lacked the spirit of Christ ... a dull dissatisfaction with the Church in high society circles ... In the more intelligent middle classes and in the lower strata of the urban population either cold indifference or even open disbelief is to be encountered.' Radstock's ministration filled this spiritual void for many. The response he found was also due to his sincerity. 'It becomes very heartening to look at him: you doubt not for one minute that this man lives in the spirit and loves other people with all his heart, and when he presses the hand of his companion and disappears into the doorway of his hotel, you feel that you have parted from the best and most sincere man of all those whom chance has led you to observe.'

Before long others took up the torch. Princess Catherine Galitsine, Countess Shouvalov, and Mme Elizabeta Chertkova, wife of the Tsar's Adjutant-General, opened many doors. Princess Galitsine was exceptional in enjoying a living faith in the Orthodox Church; others, men and women, were hungering for something more than the rituals, splendid though they were, which their Church could bring them. Russia, in fact, was being shaken by a religious as much as a political crisis. The Church had failed in its bid for a measure of freedom under Tsar Alexis in the 17th century, and had been turned into a department of state by Peter the Great in the 18th. Now, served by clergy for the most part ill-educated or even downright ignorant, it was failing to meet the devotional needs and rising spiritual aspirations of the laity, though among literate Russians some encouragement came from the first modern translation of the Bible, authorised in 1867.

The spiritual upsurge which had shaken Western Europe was also having its effect in the East, though finding channels which, for the authorities, seemed disturbingly political. Of these the most dramatic was the Populist (Narodnik) movement. In the summer of 1874, the year of Radstock's irruption into St. Petersburg society, several thousand students descended on the villages, eager 'to pay the debt' which, they believed, the educated classes owed the peasantry. Their vaguely formulated aims were to bring the peasants uplift, politicise them, and prepare the way for a new social order. 'Ethical motives played a crucial role ... Sometimes this was expressed in religious terms − a religion which gave a more or less symbolical form to their aspirations for purity and total sacrifice'. In some villages the students were accepted, but for the most part the peasants were suspicious of these urban youngsters, and sometimes reported them to the police. They were easy prey for the Third Section and other agents of government repression. Half were imprisoned, some were executed, while others were driven to madness and premature death by brutal treatment in prisons or psychiatric hospitals. The movement was broken and, for many, violent protests took the place of non-violent dissent.

An offshoot of the revivals in Britain was the activity of the British Bible Society, which had been authorised in Russia to dispense Bibles to the sectaries. A high state official, the Lord Chamberlain, Count M.M. Korff, had become committed to distributing New Testaments through visiting the British Bible Society's stand at the Paris World Exhibition of 1867, and at a similar exhibition in Russia three years later disposed of over 62,000 Bibles.

By the mid-seventies 40 aristocratic homes had opened their doors to Radstock, and he had important, though smaller, meetings in Moscow. His visit to Russia of nearly a year during the winter and summer of 1877-8 was 'the most remarkable and successful', according to his daughter Daisy, who as a child nearly died of typhus in the dark and insanitary Hôtel de France at St. Petersburg, 'filled with wounded and whole from the Russo-Turkish war' (she was one of the seven children who all came at that time with their parents, together with an elderly governess, a manservant and a nanny – 'it must have required all my father's great power of organisation to arrange this undertaking.'

Count A.P. Bobrinski, Colonel of the Corps of Nobles and Minister of Transport, was another supporter who was an influential friend at court. He had begun to look for a change in his life as a young man struck down by typhus in the Crimea. Twenty years later his meeting with Radstock made him a new man. His change interested the famous writer Leo Tolstoy – they talked together for eight hours on end until 6 a.m one night. The palace of Colonel V.A. Pashkov, owner of extensive estates and a coppermine, became the centre of the St. Petersburg work. His and other

175

ballrooms were opened to the public for meetings to which sledge-drivers, cabmen, and workers from the Putilov and other factories were as welcome as the gentry.

Among the students who came were many, who in sheer frustration at government repression, had drifted into nihilism. Students were a special care for Radstock, Pashkov and his other fellow-workers. They comprised a good proportion of the clientele frequenting the three low-cost restaurants which they established for feeding thousands daily. Those in need of food and clothing were helped — they also received tracts and Bibles. Sewing-shops and laundries were set up. 'The Society for the Encouragement of Spiritual and Ethical Reading' was formed, 'an enormous propaganda machine' which produced several million items — cards and songbooks, as well as books and brochures. At a time when literacy was spreading, this work did much to satisfy the hunger for reading matter, especially religious, which was growing among ordinary people.

Radstock's aristocratic followers brought the message to the peasants on their estates, a much more effective approach than the ill-starred students' Narodnik initiative. The large school and hospital built by Pashkov became the peasants' meeting place in his village of Krekshin. But such developments were extremely troubling to the clerical and lay defenders of the Orthodox Church's monopoly in matters of religion. Besides the 'Old Believers' who had broken away in the 17th century, other sectaries — Stundists, Molokans, Dukhobors, Baptists — had appeared. For the reactionaries of Church and State the Radstockists or Pashkovites appeared as another and even more dangerous 'sect'.

Despite their friends at Court, attempts were made to silence them. Eventually Alexander II was persuaded to expel Radstock from Russia, in 1878 — the year in which the meetings in Pashkov's huge ball-room first began seriously to attract Government attention. This was the beginning of sustained opposition led by P.K.Pobedonostzev, who in 1880 became Chief Procurator of the

Holy Synod, the committee set up by Peter the Great to control the Church. Without his aggressive and unremitting action the work of Radstock, Pashkov and their colleagues might have arrested the forces making for violent revolution by moving Russia far enough towards their aim of 'the transformation of Russia on a religious and moral basis without adhering to any specific denomination.'

About the time he assumed office, Pobedonostzev wrote to the Tsar (5 May 1880) about a conference of five and a half hours with Count Loris-Melikov, the Prime Minister in effect, and other ministers, dealing with Pashkov and his meetings. 'Everyone recognised this as a very important matter, and it was decided, without having recourse to drastic measures, to halt the meeting at once, and if Pashkov did not submit, to exile him; he and his female associates should be barred access to prisons and such institutions, and there should be close surveillance of the spreading of the propaganda of this doctrine in Russia.' This was followed a few days later with an official memorandum.

Ironically Pobedonostzev's opposition derived from his belief in the moral and spiritual basis of the State, which had to be preserved (he maintained) by safeguarding the Church's monopoly as the exponent of the only true religion, 'to the detriment of the other Churches and all other forms of worship ... [These] are not recognised as true, or at least not as entirely true'; they are regarded as inferior, and non-recognition may be reinforced by persecution. In this way the spiritual unity of State and nation is assured, its legality is respected and confidence in its power is maintained − but only if the State professes its own religion without setting itself up as impartial towards all.

In November 1880 Pobedonostzev sent another memorandum to the Tsar. Pashkov had been preaching for two years 'without permission, the Government laying no restraint on him, in contravention of the law (Art.125 of the Statute for the Prevention of Crimes) which forbids the holding of any meetings in the capital unknown to and without the approval of the Authorities.'

From preaching in a circle of upper-class friends 'he soon proceeded to address the common people. He frequented the cabmen's lodgings and other similar meeting-places of the working people. The Russian people ... assembled in great numbers to hear these sermons. Mr. Pashkov distributed among the people books [tracts] translated from foreign languages, or written in the narrow spirit of the Radstock sect.'

Meetings at his house, Pobedonostzev went on, are 'increasing week by week ... He 'throws open the splendid halls of his mansion for prayer meetings to which all who like may come ... It seems necessary without delay to put a stop to Pashkov's meetings, and to others of the same kind, and to try to prevent the spreading of the new sect, in reference to which the Church and the State, which have been undivided in Russia, cannot remain unconcerned.'

It followed (said Pobedonostzev) that Pashkov must be 'sent away from Russia, if only for a time', and Radstock must not be allowed to come on a visit. On the positive side, in order to satisfy the religious needs which drew people to Pashkov's meetings, 'it is necessary to call similar meetingss and have prayers in the spirit of the Orthodox Church with the assistance of the ablest and most zealous priests.' A special committee of the highest state officials unanimously endorsed Pobedonostzev's request to ban Pashkov's meetings, and the Governor of St.Petersburg was ordered to carry it out. At this point (March 1881) Nihilists assassinated Alexander II. Two decades of repression were the consequence, with Pobedonostzev confirmed as a leader of the reaction.

Pashkov did not give up easily. He left St.Petersburg for England, but after a few months returned to continue his missionary work on his estates and copper-mine. Pobedonostzev, who was collecting information from the bishops about the movement, urged the Minister of the Interior to enforce the anti-Pashkov order of 1880, and stop (among other things) the distribution of 'peculiar editions of the New Testament with underlined texts, hymn-books translated from the German and English, and peculiar pamphlets of Mr. Pashkov's editing – pamphlets, I am sorry to say, allowed to be printed by the Civil Censor without the knowledge of the Clerical Censor ... Among other things there is an edition of Mr. John Bunyan's *Pilgrim's Progress* with remarks of a peculiar tendency.'

Although public evangelical work in the capital had become practically impossible, for a time Pashkov and Korff continued their activity in the provinces. This was mostly among peasants belonging to the already established sects, such as Baptists and Stundists. Pashkov helped them materially, as well as supplying them with free copies of the pamphlets of the Society for the Encouragement of Spiritual and Ethical Reading. He paid unusually high wages to the several thousand workers in his copper-mine, and gave land of his own away to those that needed it. He visited peasant families in their homes, and met their requests for money, food, or building-wood. No wonder 'General Pashkov', as they called him, was popular, and that his action created the impression that the ruling powers at the capital were behind him. Had that been the case, the history of Russia and indeed of Europe might have been different, since it can be claimed that the Pashkovites were 'the only group of all social and religious societies of the 1880s which could have initiated large-scale changes within the Russian Empire.'

A growing demand among the sectaries for full religious freedom was matched by action on the part of their aristocratic well-wishers to help them become a more united body. A circular letter went out from Pashkov and Korff to the evangelical sectaries throughout Russia to assemble at St.Petersburg early in April 1884. Pashkov paid the expenses of 70 delegates, who met in his mansion and in those of Korff and Princess Lieven. It was an unforgettable experience for those who had come – many from long distances – to palaces where 'the peasant sat next to the Count and where high society ladies served the common brethren.' In the discussions, though there was unity of spirit, unity could not

179

be achieved on points of faith or ritual. The practice of Bible-study, which had led to varied interpretation of passages dealing with matters such as the breaking of bread, the sacraments and particularly baptism, showed its effects in the varieties of practice. After long sittings it was agreed to differ, and focus instead on ethical questions. But the planned ten days of the conference could not be completed. After five days the police moved in and arrested the provincial delegates. All the efforts of Pashkov and Korff failed to obtain their release, and after two days in prison they were packed on to trains and sent back home.

The conference was the signal for further repression of the movement. A month later the Society for the Encouragement of Spiritual and Ethical Reading was officially dissolved, meetings were prohibited, and homes where prayer-meetings took place were put under surveillance, threatened by searches and arrests. Pobedonostzev presented a voluminous anti-Pashkov dossier to Alexander III, who requested that Pashkov and Korff should sign a pledge never again to preach or take part in Bible-reading on pain of banishment. This they refused to do, and (except for one brief visit permitted to Pashkov) spent the rest of their lives in exile.

Although activity on Pashkovite lines continued among the peasantry, the movement was effectively terminated. Peasants arraigned by the authorities tended to mask their adherence, and allied themselves with the larger sects. Those that admitted their involvement were evicted from their homes or banished to remote areas, forced to march in chains like criminals. Often children were separated from their parents.

'It was obvious that the banishment for religious convictions by 'the Supreme Court of Appeal', the Emperor, [had] a stagger-ing demoralizing effect on the minds of many aristocrats.' Pobedonostzev had demonstrated that freedom in matters of faith and practice enjoyed by aristocrats in their drawing-rooms could not be extended to peasants, nor could the aristocrats any longer have such freedom in their homes. The punishment of two members of the court nobility might well be followed by similar harshness towards others of the aristocracy. Most of the Pashkovite aristocracy sank into a life of impotent frustration. The exceptions were the three 'Tsar's widows', as they were called, Mme Chertkova, Princess Gagarina and Princess Lieven, who invited preachers from the Stundists and Baptists, but the effect was merely to merge what was left of Radstock's legacy with the doctrines and practices of these other sects.

Pobedonostzev had won, at the cost of depriving Russia of the kind of moral and spiritual revival which in Britain, through the Evangelical and associated movements, had in the early 19th century helped to turn revolutionary aspirations into constitutional channels of social and political reform. His positive achievement had been to stimulate a revival of the Orthodox Church by specially trained missioners, and by encouraging the innovation of sermons related to practical life. This opened the way to the movement at the turn of the century described as Russia's 'religious renaissance', which however came too late to forestall the imposition by the Bolsheviks of Marxism-Leninism as the monopolistic replacement of Orthodoxy.

'Through what throes the nation must yet pass, by what ordeals the living Church, imprisoned within her dead forms, shall yet shake herself free, and arise from the dust, time alone can declare; all that is at present clear is that the bonds of centuries are riven.' So wrote Lord Radstock's biographer a few years after these events, in 1905 while the first of Russia's 20th century revolutions was shaking the Empire. Radstock meanwhile had remained faithful to his calling. Expelled from Russia in 1878, he had proceeded with his family to Stockholm, at the invitation of Queen Sophie and notables, where a revival of St. Petersburg dimensions took place. 'There are certain times, I believe,' he wrote, 'when the Word of God speaks not only to individuals, but to a whole community.' This was followed by similar invitations and similar events in Finland, Denmark and Holland.

The pattern of his life continued over the years, whether in the austere surroundings of his English home, in the Viceregal Palace at Calcutta, or in the modest hotel at Paris, where he had often stayed (though without a fire in his bedroom even in winter, for the sake of economy). From there he took part in evangelical meetings in the city, and it was there that he died in December 1913. A few months later the Great War broke out, the first of those catastrophes of which 'he had warned men unceasingly, especially during the later years of his life', as about to shake 'a too pleasure-loving, material society' — though he never abandoned hope that, through this suffering, purification and regeneration might result.

REFERENCES (page references for quotations in order of appearance):

Mrs.Edward Trotter: *Lord Radstock* (London 1914),15,14,184-5,188,23,248; *Undertones of the 19th Century* (London 1905), 44,47,48,46*ff*,53,103.

W.T.Stead: *The Truth about Russia* (London 1888),356 (in Swiss train).

P.K.Pobedonostzev: *Questions religieuses, sociales et politiques* (Paris 1897),16.

E.Heier: *Religious Schism in the Russian Aristocracy 1860-1900* (The Hague 1970),based mainly on Pobedonostzev's correspondence and other Russian sources), 118,6,126-9,133, 136,137,146.

K.P.Pobedonostzev and his correspondence (Moscow 1921, in Russian), letter of 5 May 1880, no.224,p.284.

R.S.Latimer: *Dr.Baedeker and his Apostolic Work in Russia* (London 1907).

Daisy Bevan (Mrs.Edwyn Bevan, née Mary Waldegrave): *Odd memories of an ordinary person* (unpublished).

Franco Venturi: *Roots of Revolution* (New York 1966),473-4

J.H.Billington: *The Icon and the Axe* (London 1966).

Anatole Leroy-Beaulieu: *L'Empire des Tsars et les Russes* (Paris 1881).

Nicholas Zernov: *The Russian Religious Renaissance of the Twentieth Century* (London 1963).

Nikolai Leskov: *Schism in High Society* (St.Petersburg 1877, tr.James Muckle, Bramcote Press, Nottingham 1995), 72,76*ff*,82,92,101.

A TIME OF QUIET

By Dr. Charis Waddy,
author of *The Muslim Mind*
and *Women in Muslim History*

There is no method, but there are certain elements. An hour before breakfast is the preferred time, while the mind is fresh. Writing down thoughts aids clarity. Aspects I find essential include the following:

1) THANKS: Gratitude is a vital orientation, essential in personal relationships as well as in relation to God.

2) PERSPECTIVE: To pray for something or someone right outside my own immediate concerns broadens what can be a very narrow circle of concern.

3) WHAT TO DO: This involves orders for the day; and also special decisions or problems. When I am obsessed by a problem, I seldom seem to get a direct answer to it. But afterwards the whole question simplifies itself. I may have to leave the matter in God's hands; or I see what to do or what *not* to do. Blocks such as self-importance or sentimentality may have to clear away.

4) FOOD FOR THE SPIRIT: A health-giving diet is needed, counteracting the plentiful amounts of despair, cynicism and dirt provided by much of the reading and viewing matter of the day. The Bible and other treasuries of faith, other books, news, letters − all these feed the spirit and help us to feed others.

5) TIMELESSNESS: At some point, time needs to be forgotten and the troubles and fascinations of the day be allowed to drop away. The shift is from 'what to do' to what God is doing. And with it comes the gift of a sense of worth, of loving and being loved, of respect for my own calling and that of those around me. In this perspective, I can think of others and their needs, put myself into their shoes and receive insight and understanding which in my own nature I totally lack. Also I find the humility to

carry out the simple, unspectacular tasks which a calling to follow God's way usually involves.

But more often than a sense of worth, there comes a sense of worthlessness, of guilt, the *sense of sin*. Inadequacy, powerlessness, dirt, adding up to 'I'm no good'. How to cope with this?

Modern psychologists try to get rid of the sense of guilt, rather than washing away the sin. There is an attraction in this. When my conscience talks, my pride is hurt. Why should I once again be shown to be so feeble, when I long to be so strong, wise and above all well thought of? Personally I have stopped agonising over my frequent misdeeds, not because of psychology but perhaps because of the dawn of some measure of humility. I cannot remember who first said to me, 'What can you expect of a pig but a grunt?' I ask forgiveness both for the pride and the misdeed, and try not to waste time off track.

A time of quiet is available for anyone, anywhere, in any circumstances. There are two conditions: the willingness to seek God's will rather than my own, and to test my behaviour by absolute moral standards. As T.S. Eliot put it, the gift is free — costing not less than everything.

APPENDIX 3

INTERFAITH APPROACHES

1. Extracts from *A Christian approach to other faiths* by Michael Hutchinson (Grosvenor Books, London 1991).

To mend any broken relationship I have to start with myself. No one can evade this, least of all those whose Master has said, 'Blessed are the peacemakers for they shall be called God's sons.' We bear a heavy entail. For many generations, while claiming to be Christians, we have put our real faith in our wealth, our arms, our technology. In spite of the missionaries and saints, the dedicated doctors and teachers, the overwhelming aspect of our Western culture has been materialist. Even when the days of empire are over, the attitudes of imperialism hang on, the deep sense of our superiority, so much part of us that we do not know it is there.

What makes it worse is that this is compounded by our picture of our religion. We think of ourselves as superior because we subscribe to its teaching and belong to its institutions. What is wrong with a view of Christianity that has made us not more humble but more proud?

From the very outset of his public ministry, Jesus laid down the marker that the love of God was for all people and not just the chosen few. The writers of the New Testament, while seeing a contrast between Moses and Christ, saw a pattern for the believer in Abraham's faith. From his side it consisted in a costly and adventurous following of God's summons and commands. In spite of disobedience, in the end he obeyed concerning all that was dearest to him, and as he obeyed God gave him insight into the divine ways and purposes.

This truth we can appreciate only if we wholeheartedly put ourselves at God's disposal to obey and follow. Here we stand on the same footing as the other children of Abraham and with every seeker after truth, as servants like them, called to obey more sensitively and selflessly than we have done hitherto.

There is much to learn from those schooled in other faiths. I have found it painful to be reminded of wrongs done in the name of Christ: persecutions, crusades, the long and shameful history of antisemitism and – closer to home – hurtful attitudes of effortless superiority. Repenting of these things I recalled the words of the prophet, 'What does the Lord require of you but ... to walk humbly with your God' (Micah 6 v 8).

Before that approach barriers of mistrust vanish. Often the Asian is more ready to listen to 'the inner voice', which the Westerner has silenced with his brain. The presence of Buddhist teachers may stimulate us to turn from superficial activism to the quest for silence and self-knowledge. We can be grateful to the Muslims with their deep sense of the Creator, a sense which allows no division between the sacred and the secular.

Prayers unite. A Parsee couple in India were deeply moved when Christian priests, their friends, said prayers and Masses for the husband when he was dangerously ill.

Denunciations divide, gratitude expressed builds bridges. We have seen Rabbi Blue on the television screen singing a Yiddish song in the church where Bede prayed thirteen centuries ago, and thanking God for the English heritage of faith. We no less can acknowledge our debt to the Jews whom Pope John Paul II has called 'our older brothers', who teach us to wait patiently on God: 'Morning by morning he wakens me. He wakens my ear to hear like those who are taught' (Isaiah 50 v 4).

We can also thank them for giving the world an idea more needed for our survival than any other today. One of them conceived the oldest story about forgiveness in the world's literature, the story of Joseph sold by jealous brothers into slavery in Egypt. It ends, 'Joseph kissed all his brothers and wept upon them' (Genesis 45 v 15).

The Spirit of truth takes each of us where we are. He has surprised me with an unexpected sense of wonder and gratitude, or of shame, with a warning of danger, even with a calling to a life-work. He may drop a thought in my mind – an apology, something to put right, the thought to care for someone towards whom the heart has grown cold. Such experiences, whatever a person's background of belief or unbelief, may be the first glimpse of God coming down to humanity.

Mysteriously present, the Holy Spirit slips past defences, prejudices and preconceived ideas, evasions and refusals. The world wants to know how Christians have obeyed, for what we have been forgiven, what that guide means to us. The world wants to know in what way the ancient prayer to the Holy Spirit is answered:

> Wash away the dirt;
> Water the dry places;
> Heal the wounds;
> Bend the rigid mind;
> Warm the cold heart;
> Direct the wayward will.

> (From the 13th century hymn, *Veni, Sancte Spiritus*, attributed to Stephen Langton, Archbishop of Canterbury).

The holiness of the Spirit, the purity He offers, goes far beyond trying to keep a high standard for oneself. It means allowing the deepest emotions, passions and affections to be purified and redirected and creatively used in the care of people and the battles to be fought over great issues.

Instead of making plans, however excellent, and asking God to bless them, Bishop John Taylor urges us to 'begin in the beginning with the Holy Spirit. This means humbly watching in any situation in which we find ourselves in order to learn what God is trying to do, and then doing it with him.'

What is God trying to do?

A reconciliation of the divided children of Abraham, Jewish, Christian and Muslim? A healing of fierce hatred, let loose as dictatorships crumble? A shock to Western democracies as those emerging from communism bring home to us that they look to us for something better than our decay of family life, rising crime and the 'blame-game' of politics?

Yet God seems to be offering us something more basic than the solving of our problems, a chance to pioneer in the fulfilment of Jesus's prediction, 'It is written in the prophets, 'And they shall all be taught by God.''(John 6 v 45; Isaiah 54 v 13).

2. Extracts from a Lent address at Liverpool Parish Church by Dr. Omnia Marzouk, a Consultant Paediatrician at the Royal Liverpool Children's Hospital, March 1997.

Thank you for inviting me to contribute to this series of Lent addresses. This is a special time of fasting, prayer and reflection for the Christian community, so I am aware that it takes a very generous and open spirit to invite someone of a different faith tradition to share in it.

'We have made you different nations and tribes that you may get to know one another. The noblest among you in the sight of Allah is he who is best in conduct.' This statement from the Koran implies that our diversity and differences are part of God's mysterious tapestry. Some people fear this diversity will fragment our society. I personally feel it is a great gift and can be a creative force in the world.

You have to see history through the eyes of others – realising the legacy that history has left in people. This was brought home to me when I travelled around India with a group of Christian and Hindu friends during the Gulf War. At the time I was full of strong feelings about the injustice of the war, the West's portrayal of Arabs and Islam and a resurgence of much antagonism towards us. In India I was confronted with the fact that when the Muslim Moguls invaded India they left a trail of wrong deeds and hurts that continue to inflame division and conflict in India today. I was made aware that some of my Christian companions had been deeply hurt by the encounters with the Muslim world.

Suddenly I saw that there was another side to the coin — that there were times when 'my group' was inflicting pain on others. 'My group' was not blameless. How much I was hurt and how I felt were no longer the essential questions — but was I prepared to live differently enough to bring healing and reconciliation? I realised I had to be free of anger, resentment and fears to be able to contribute to new understanding between our differing communities.

But I also had to accept the legacy of history, and hope that a sincerely expressed apology for that past was a vital step towards reconciliation. In the group I was travelling with I was given the chance to apologise to Hindus and Christians who had been hurt by their encounters with Islam. This built trust between the Hindu and Muslim communities we met.

I feel we are all called to live our faith at two levels. The personal and the global dimensions cannot be separated. Much is said about the need for a moral regeneration in this country, but this cannot be enforced from outside. We all have to live differently — a decision to lift the veil that sometimes separates the theory of our faith from what we live out day to day. Can we each face squarely the legacy of our inherited history? Can we each acknowledge where it has inflicted wrong on others? Can we express sincere apology for that and make some concrete act of restitution? This is the key to reconciliation.

However reconciliation is not an end in itself. It is a means to a more important end. Through true reconciliation, people of all faith traditions working together will then be a force that can make a difference. In the world context there is so much that we can tackle together: poverty, environment, rich/poor gap to name but a few. On the home front we could just start by making sure that in the next decades Britain becomes a true home for all who live on its shores and where no-one feels marginalised or excluded.

3. André Chouraqui, writing from Jerusalem, believes that the message of the prophets is more relevant than ever. Their ideas have become a necessity if mankind is to continue to exist. 'A new man will be born', or rather 'a new type of men', of whom the prototypes are the prophets of old.

It is not 'progress' that the prophets announce, but 'a cosmic mutation which will set the universe and Man in accord with the law of life and creation.' For us it *is* a 'mutation' perhaps, in our character and motives, which enables us to come nearer that moral level of living expressed by Chouraqui as being 'transparent towards God and men, cleansed of all dirt so that the light coming from on high can penetrate and illuminate us.'

How has he reached these convictions? His ancestral faith was destroyed in the atheistic atmosphere of the lycée, but he began to recover his faith through two young Protestant nurses training for the mission-field. While he was in hospital for a time, they interested him in the Bible. Then he undertook Hebrew studies at Paris, where professors and rabbis greatly deepened his understanding of his spiritual patrimony. Also he learned much from the Sufis of Southern Algeria (his native land). His recovery of faith took place in a super-ecumenical way: he writes of 'the shock of discovering God by way of Christian and Muslim spirituality.'

Already before the war Chouraqui had foreseen that there would be 'unheard-of destruction' as a consequence of the conflict which was about to take place. He felt himself, along with so many other Jews, to be nailed on the cross by the persecutors – 'the same cross on which the Roman Empire crucified the peoples who dared to resist its law.' At this moment he saw it would be necessary to start 'a revolutionary action which would alter the course of history'. With this vision, he says, 'another self was born in me ... I learnt for the first time to see evil in myself in contrast with the absolute of perfection.' He understood that 'it would be necessary to found a new order whose roots would reach down into the still living depths of Israel, of Christianity, and of Islam ... The nearer we get back to our sources the nearer we will be to each other, without ceasing to be intensely ourselves.'

One of his deepest experiences took place after the Vichy government deprived him of his French citizenship and his right to practise his profession as a lawyer. He entered the Resistance (the Maquis), in a unit in which 'bearded maquisards' in their off-duty time 'studied their Hebrew Bible' and other scriptures (of this group only he and one other survived the war). It was during this period that he understood that the greatest revolution which is taking place in the world is 'the revolution of silence'.

My spirit became more and more attentive to the contemplation of the Creator. A certain kind of silence sometimes makes possible the revealing of God's presence and his voice. While the world was crumbling in the fracas of war, I discovered this new realm which our ancestors indicated in giving us instructions to make silence within ourselves and to listen: 'Hear, O Israel!'

Huddled in my solitary places, I tried to practise this instruction, to make silence, not only with my mouth but with all my other senses. I tried also to make myself so small, so receptive, that I could attain the silence of the mind: to stop in myself the flow of ideas and of images that made a screen between my own tumult and the uncreated ocean of silence. There, sometimes I felt such a powerful communion that it ended by conquering my poor humanity. It certainly seemed then that, in the quiet knowledge of my nothingness, I experienced the sovereign presence of a personal God of unity and love.

192

Chouraqui's hope is the spiritual reawakening of humanity, in face of the danger of 'universal suicide' – a restoration which will draw its energies from 'the sources of silence. I am expecting men to arise,' he says, 'fully attentive to silence, and present at the zero hour of humanity.'

(Adapted from an article in the London *Times* of 6 August 1983). Quotations are from *Ce que je crois; Lettre à un ami arabe*; *Lettre à un ami chrétien; Retour aux racines*. More recent writing includes his autobiography *L'Amour fort comme la mort*. He has also published translations into French from the original languages of the Bible and the Koran, and an illustrated commentary on the Bible in ten volumes, *L'Univers de la Bible)*.

After the war he practised as a lawyer in Algeria before moving to Jerusalem where he became a deputy mayor with Teddy Kollek, eventually resigning in order to devote himself to writing and translation work. Shimon Peres wrote the Preface to *Lettre à un ami arabe* (English translation, Amherst, U.S.A. 1972).

4. 'Mahatma Gandhi was no Christian, and the Christians were amazed that this should be so, for never in modern times had they seen any man tread more faithfully in the footsteps of Christ. Whence did he derive his astonishing strength? ... Gandhi did not see himself primarily as the architect of Indian independence from British rule but as the liberator of the Indian spirit from the fetters of greed and anger, hatred and despair. In his frail person the ancient ideals of renunciation, 'harmlessness' (*ahimsa,* translated by him as 'non-violence'), and truth met. He described himself as a *sanatani* Hindu, one who follows the *sanatana dharma-raja* ... He had before his eyes too the Aya Samaj of Dayananda whose interpretation of the Veda was so utterly at variance with that of the orthodox that plainly one could do with the sacred texts almost anything one liked. So it seemed only natural that he could say of the scriptures, 'My belief in the Hindu Scriptures does not require

me to accept every word and every verse as divinely inspired. Nor do I claim to have any first-hand knowledge of these wonderful books. But I do claim to know and feel the truths of the essential teaching of the Scriptures. I decline to be bound by any interpretation, however learned it may be, if it is repugnant to reason and moral sense.' ... 'To me God is Truth and Love; *God is ethics and morality;* God is fearlessness; God is the source of Light and Life, and yet he is above and beyond all these. *God is conscience.*' God is, in fact, what Gandhi in his heart feels him to be: he is not the God of the law-books or even of the Vedas, should these prove to conflict with the light within him.' (R.C.Zaehner: *Hinduism,* Oxford 1966,pp.170-2).

'I was simply overjoyed' with the Sermon on the Mount, Gandhi said, when he first came across it, in London when he was there in 1888-9. (Rajmohan Gandhi: *The Good Boatman, a Portrait of Gandhi*, Viking,New Delhi and London 1995,p.8). During this London period reading 'Arnold's *Light of Asia* had a similar effect and taught him about the Buddha ... and he read Carlyle on the Prophet of Islam.' He also joined the Anjuman-e-Islamia, an association of Muslim students. (Ibid.,61)

'Like David [in the Bible], Gandhi was aware of enemies plotting to kill him. Both prayed from their depths, David for deliverance from his foes, Gandhi for the ability to do or die and for goodwill towards his killers. The name of God, Rama in Gandhi's case, meant much to both. David sang with burning sincerity − 'David's psalms transport you to raptures,' Gandhi wrote in 1926 ... If he partook of David, he also ... partook of Krishna. 'He was a friend and lover of all the men and women he met,' said Rajagopalachari, adding, 'Indeed he was like Krishna.'' (ibid.,454-5). 'Asked in Lausanne in December 1931, 'What is truth?' Gandhi answered : 'A difficult question, but I have solved it for myself by saying that it is what the voice within tells me.' ... In 1933 he remarked that to him 'the voice of God, of conscience, of truth, or the inner voice or the still small voice means one and the same thing ... Whatever or Whosoever this voice was 'I have been a willing slave to this most exacting Master for more than half a century.' ... Eleven years earlier he had declared that 'the only tyrant I accept in this world is the still small voice within'. (Ibid.,202) ... Gandhi doggedly sought to make [nationalism] as righteous as possible ... and to treat Indian independence as only the stepping-stone to a new world.' (Ibid.,87).

Another observation by Gandhi was: 'As my contact with real Christians, that is men living in fear of God, increased, I saw the Sermon on the Mount was the whole Christianity for him who wanted to live a Christian life. It is that sermon which endeared Jesus to me.'

He was asked, 'What is the most effective way of preaching the Gospel of Christ?' to which he replied:
'To live the gospel is the most effective way — most effective in the beginning, in the middle and in the end ... But I love those who never preach, but live according to their lights'. (M.K.Gandhi: *The Message of Jesus Christ,* Bharatiya Vidya Bhavan, Bombay 1964).

5. Lord Rees-Mogg reminded readers of the London *Times* that the spiritual inspiration through faith 'flows in loving actions towards other people'. Christians see in Jesus 'a perfect identity' between that which is inner and spiritual — 'the divine spirit' — and the 'outward life of action ... All the world's religions express this relationship in their own way' ... It is the loving actions which count in a life of prayer. The words of the aged Apostle John in his last sermon were simply 'little children, love one another'. This is also the aim of the Jewish religion, of Islam, of Buddhism, particularly in the high form of Tibetan Buddhism, of Sikhism and of contemplative Hinduism. In this sense at least, all the religions have a common purpose and may be compared to different telescopes which look up at the same night sky. No doubt the

telescopes are different; some may be more powerful or better focused than others. If human beings are in touch with what Buddhists would call 'the wisdom mind' and Christians 'the Holy Spirit' — the two concepts are not doctrinally identical — they will be naturally impelled to good deeds.' (22/3/93).

ROME AND THE
DESTRUCTION OF JERUSALEM

There may have been a possibility of a promising change in the relations of Jews and Romans if the precept of Jesus to love one's enemies had been applied by enough people. He showed the way in his healing of the centurion's servant and and by his commending of the centurion's faith (Matthew 8 vs 5-18). Jews friendly to Romans, with reciprocity, are depicted in Luke's account of the same event: the 'elders of the Jews' whom the centurion sent to Jesus 'besought him instantly, saying, That he was worthy for whom he should do this, for he loves our nation and he has built us a synagogue' (Luke 7 vs 3-5). After the Crucifixion, Peter developed this relation to Romans further by responding to the appeal of the centurion Cornelius, a God-fearer and friendly to the Jews, by going with a party of the brethren to the army HQ at Caesarea where he expounded the Gospel message and baptised Cornelius with the 'kinsmen and near friends' whom he had gathered for the occasion (Acts ch.10).

It is true that the Sadducees were something like a pro-Roman party, formed from aristocratic families who enjoyed the power and prestige of appointments such as that of High Priest, and who dominated the council concerned with religious affairs, the Sanhedrin. At the other end of the scale were the Zealots (fundamentalist nationalists). There were also non-political extremists, notably the Essenes, who lived unto themselves in their Dead Sea monasteries. The Pharisees were also entirely concerned with religious matters, but were themselves divided into two parties, one composed of the followers of Hillel, a rabbinic teacher of the generation before Jesus, 'advocates of mildness and tolerance in the interpretation and carrying out of legal precepts,' the other being followers of Shammai, 'hard, rigid and exacting'. The denunciations by Jesus of the 'Pharisees', apparently of the Shammaite wing, indicate the strong feelings and mutual antagonisms among the Jewish parties at Jerusalem which made any general move of reconciliation with the Roman occupiers difficult or impossible.

Under incompetent or provocative Roman governors, such as Pontius Pilate, these antagonisms developed into open hostility among the different parties. The nationalists, ignoring pressure from the moderate elements, incited open war against the Romans, while exacerbating the rifts with and within the rest of the population of Jerusalem. 'Every community, every family, was divided against itself by those who clamoured for war and those who demanded peace.' The Zealots gained the upper hand and carried out a reign of terror. 'Vespasian waited for two years until the Judeans, weakened by their internal strife, should be entirely at his mercy.' When his son Titus took over the command of the Roman army from his father Vespasian, he offered peace by negotiating terms of submission. This was refused, and after a terrible siege Jerusalem was destroyed along with the Temple in 70 CE. (Quotations from *A New Commentary on Holy Scripture*, edited by C. Gore, H.L.Goudge and A.Guillaume, SPCK, London 1929, pp.18,19, and H.Graetz: *History of the Jews*, London 1891,vol.2, chapters 7 and 11. See also Josephus: *The Jewish War;* J.S.Riggs: *A History of the Jewish People*, vol.4, London 1908; Joseph Klausner: *Jesus of Nazareth*, trans. H. Danby, London n.d.,?1925; pp.216ff.; C.H.Dodd: *The Founder of Christianity*, London 1971, pp.77-8, quotes Klausner,p.376 with comments.)

THE CHEMISTRY OF A GRAND DESIGN

by Dr.Alwyn McKay,
Principal Scientific Officer at the Atomic Energy
Research Establishment, Harwell, 1948-1980.
Author of *The Making of the Atomic Age*

The traditional argument from design for the existence of God may have been killed by Darwinism, but in a changed form it is still very much alive. Darwin's concept of evolution through natural selection undermined William Paley's proposition in *Natural Theology* that the fitness of organisms for their various environments implies an intelligent, beneficent designer, but many scientists today are turning to the obverse of Paley's idea: what still needs to be explained is the extraordinary fitness of the natural world as a vehicle for life, which in turn depends on the characteristics of the cosmos.

It is primarily the physicists and cosmologists who have made the running here. They have been deeply impressed by the fine-tuning of many physical quantities that is necessary to produce a universe like ours. There is a delicate balance in, for instance, the strengths of the fundamental forces, or the stability of protons and neutrons, without which there would probably be no galaxies, no stars, no temperate planet like the Earth, no wide range of chemical elements, and hence no life.

Stephen Hawking in *A Brief History of Time* says that some cosmological theories seem almost to imply 'the act of a God who intended to create beings like us ...'

Less attention is paid to chemistry in this connection, yet it is more directly relevant to life than is physics. Most of the universe is too hot or too cold for much in the way of chemical processes. Atoms only begin to form molecules below say 5,000C, [at temperatures] far lower than those of most of the objects visible in a telescope, while complicated biological molecules can only survive for long at temperatures as low as those of our own Earth.

When temperatures fall still further, everything freezes and chemistry comes to a halt. It follows that chemical design arguments will be concerned with what goes on under the temperate conditions we experience daily ...

At the risk of over-simplifying, it could be said that the physics must be right for the universe to produce the appropriate range of chemical elements, and ... for those elements to produce life as we know it. (*The Times*, 28/8/89)

APPENDIX 6

PERSONAL CHANGE

What happens when a person changes? Can there be a 'revolutionary' change in a person's nature?

The classic on this subject, William James' *The Varieties of Religious Experience,* was the product of the same spiritual and intellectual climate which saw the flowering of the campus movement at the turn of the century. A person who experiences this shift in his spiritual centre, says James, differs from his previous self in perfectly definite ways – 'temptations may remain completely annulled ... as if by alteration of a man's habitual nature.' He cites comments of those who had this experience: 'in one year my whole nature was changed ... a vivid realisation of forgiveness and renewal of my nature ... a profound modification of my nature, a new manner of my being.' (Edition of 1902, 267-269,252,249,271n.)

James summarises this making of 'a new man, a new creature', as 'shiftings of character to higher levels', and 'an irreversible revolution.' His description of the usual form in which events take place leading to this experience is: '1. An uneasiness; and 2. its solution. The uneasiness ... is a sense that there is something wrong about us as we naturally stand. The solution is a sense that we are saved from the wrongness by making proper connection with the higher powers.'

Frank Buchman suggested an experimental time of quiet. 'Have you ever tried taking pencil and paper, and writing down the thoughts that come to you? They may look like ordinary thoughts. But be honest about them. You might get a new picture of yourself. Absolute honesty, absolute purity, absolute unselfishness, absolute love. Those are Christ's standards. Are they yours? You may have to put things straight. I had to. I began by writing to six people, admitting that ill-will between us was my fault, and not theirs. Then I could really help people. Remember – if you want the world to get straight, get straight yourself.' (Buchman, op.cit.,40).

This experience is valid for young as for old. A Swedish girl said, 'Purity gives you a sparkle which does not have to be put on. It satisfies you deep down. Permissiveness, instead of satisfying, just makes you grab for more and more. Purity and care for others go together in my life and that is why I think it is progressive.' (Sidney Cook and Garth Lean: *The Black and White Book,* London 1972).

The effects of such experiences, as William James says, 'might conceivably transform the world'. (p.283)

A former atheist recently described her experience as finding herself in what she could only describe as 'a sea of sparkling energy ... a limitless ocean of consciousness ... the source of everything in existence from the largest planet to the smallest insect, ... a feeling of coming home in the fullest sense, of finally knowing one's true nature, because everything we experience, from joy, love and acts of genius to pain, grief and destruction – all come from this source. And knowing this has taught me to be grateful for every breath.' (Catherine Lucas in *The Times*, London, 24/12/97).

Author's note: In such matters one's own experience is decisive. Ms.Lucas came to hers initially by three weeks among the 'awe-inspiring ... magnificence of the rocks, the trees, the mountains [of Oregon] and the light above them, so shatteringly clear.' Many have found in the beauties of nature the beginnings of their discovery of God. In my case, when a student of 19, the pattern of my experience was similar to that of William James, taking the form of occasional depression and a sense of futility. This led me to look for a philosophy of life which would keep me going through difficult as well as good times. I began to find this by seriously reading the Bible for the first time, being struck by the verse in Luke 11 v.9: 'knock and it will be opened unto you, seek and you will find.' And progressively this was the case, while

I observed and then rejected the fashionable 'isms, communism and fascism. A personal 'answer' to the problems of living became part of a growing understanding of the oncoming decadence of our culture, illuminated by Albert Schweitzer's lectures which he was currently giving at Oxford on the theme of his book *The Decay and the Restoration of Civilisation.*

'As Schweitzer says,' I wrote home, 'civilisation is breaking up faster than ever. It won't need another war to show us *that.* It is very interesting drawing analogies from the Hitler régime showing how it militates in every way against the essential conditions for restoring civilisation ... It is now possible to understand the great minds of Imperial Roman decadence, seeing the *inevitable collapse* of civilisation, seeing it and being quite impotent to stop it ... But I still think there's hope – just a chance – and I think Schweitzer does too.' (RCM, 22/10/1933)

Even after another world war and the continuance of precarious conditions in the world, that chance miraculously remains.

As well as the initial change, or the acceptance of an unquestioning faith through being brought up in a believing and practising home, deeper experiences of change (or its maturing) may come later, as in the case of Luther, Wesley and many others, among them Søren Kierkegaard. 1848 was a key year both in the life of Kierkegaard and in European history. 'The year of revolutions' also saw a revolution in his life. After years of faith and attempting to live it, he had a 'profound transformation which made this year the most productive of his life.' (Walter Lowrie: *A Short Life of Kierkegaard*, Princeton 1965), 201. The previous August he had abandoned a visit to Berlin because he felt impelled to 'come to myself in a deeper sense, by coming closer to God in the understanding of myself. I must remain on the spot *and be renewed inwardly.*' (Lowrie,203) He had been suffering from depression and a sense of the sinfulness of his past life, aggravated by material insecurity and the hostility of the press, when he was transformed, convinced not only that God had forgiven him, but that He had even 'forgotten' his sins. 'When a man has thus verily experienced, and experiences what it is to believe in the forgiveness of his sins,' he wrote, 'he has certainly become another man.' (Lowrie,207)

This was the outcome of 'the humiliation, which will drive most men to despair, of enduring to be a single person ... to have to stand alone, forsaken, scorned and ridiculed.' (Kierkegaard: *The Last Years, Journals 1853-55,* ed. and trans. R.Gregor Smith, Fontana 1968,355) Being a Christian is not just assenting to a doctrine: 'no, God, who knows the scoundrel that man is, aims at something else — at transforming character.' (Ibid.,275) 'Christianity in the New Testament has to do with man's will, everything turns upon changing the will..Everything is related to this basic idea in Christianity which makes it what it is — a change of will.' (Ibid.,226)

It was this change in his life which brought Kierkegaard to his strongest attack on ordinary church-going Christianity. Because at that time culture and society in the West were so much the product of Christian ideas and practices, an attack on contemporary 'Christianity' was an attack on society in general. But the failure of Christianity was endangering society itself. 'This land is morally decayed.' (Ibid.,89) 'Everyone who has a little experience knows at heart that this is a rotten world.' (Ibid.,101)

One of Kierkegaard's parables was about geese who could talk.

Every Sunday they came together, and a gander preached. The essential content of the sermon was: what a lofty destiny the goose had, what a high goal the Creator (and every time his name was mentioned the geese curtised and the ganders bowed their heads) had set before the goose; by the aid of wings it could fly away to distant regions, blessed climes, where properly it was at home, for it was only a stranger here. So it was every Sunday, and that was the end of it ... They throve and were well-liking, became plump and delicate — and then were eaten on Martinmas Eve.

Then a wild goose arrived who encouraged the geese 'to rise a little higher, and then a little higher, with the hope that that they might be able to follow the flock [of wild geese] liberated from this pitiable life of mediocrity, waddling on the ground as respectable tame geese.' But he failed — for by now the tame geese had power over him. He stayed on, and 'the end of the story was that the wild goose became a tame goose.' (Lowrie,258)

Kierkegaard was pessimistic about a tame goose becoming a wild one, 'but on the other hand a wild goose can certainly become a tame goose — watch out!' (Lowrie,258)

EPILOGUE

One of the most thoughtful successors to Martin Wight in regard to possible better functioning of international relations is K.N. Waltz. He presents three aspects in which this can be analysed:

(1) The 'improvement' of persons —changing human nature;

(2) improvements within the structures of states;

(3) improvements in the system of states' relations to each other.[1]

In regard to the first aspect or 'image' he says 'if changing human nature will solve the problem, then one has to discover how to bring about the change.'[2] Such a change is the aim of those who believe that 'human behaviour...is determined more by religious-spiritual inspiration than by material circumstance' — but he views this approach as unrealistic since it does not take sufficently into account 'the influence of social and political institutions.' The rapacity of men, he opines, has to be controlled by force rather than 'exhortations'.[3]

But it is a legitimate hope that a creative minority of men and women who have experienced change in their nature or character can initiate improvements in human relations, starting with themselves, which can then promote improvements in 'images' 2 and 3. Despite the scepticism of Professor Waltz ('war will be perpetually associated with the existence of separate sovereign states'[4]), in this Epilogue the reader can be reminded that the initiatives of European statesmen since 1945 *have* forged a new unity between formerly war-torn nations, and that the principles of peaceful change, on which this success was based, open the way to peaceful change in the relations of other states throughout the world.

The spiritual context in which these changes took place was the Christian faith. Assuming this to be the first stage in a process affecting other countries, the spiritual context must be interfaith. The world's great religions should find a new dynamic together, as more reconciliation is effected between the different branches and sects into which they have become divided. The Power, transcendent and immanent, creator and sustainer of the Universe, by whatever name we call it, continues 'to work its purpose out as year succeeds to year', through people of all faiths everywhere.

At the same time the 'international anarchy' (as it is called) has been modified by bringing all viable states into the United Nations, which – thanks in part to its upbuilding by Dag Hammerskjöld – has not suffered a decline like that of the League of Nations in the 1930s, when some of the European 'great powers' set themselves up as a directorate[5] in its place under leaders who had neither the moral qualities nor the insight to deal with Mussolini and Hitler.

Now the United States has become the only superpower after effecting the Soviet Union's collapse by *cold* warfare (another 'first' of the 20th century), bringing states formerly part of the Soviet Empire, as well as Russia itself, under its hegemony. America's reach however is not fully global, since the situation may come once more into a balance,[6] this time of America (as the West-based hegemon) with China and its satellites. Now in the Nuclear Age, with mutual annihilation as the probable consequence of full-scale war, the new developments in conflict resolution under the auspices of the U.N. on a hopefully sound moral and spiritual basis, should be the preferred option by all concerned. Can we humans move beyond the concept of 'balance of power', not only between states but between hegemonies? Going back to the early centuries of the first Millennium CE, must we reproduce the pattern of the Roman Empire versus that of Persia with all their continual wars? Instead the harmonious equilibrium of the three main cultural areas of Western Eurasia – Islam, Byzantium and Latin Christendom – as it existed at the start of our now expiring millennium, is a pattern to be restored, not again to be broken (it may be hoped) by a Huntingtonian clash of civilisations, as that one was, by the barbaric incursion of the Crusades into the Islamic area.

But to get from our present disordered world to one of peace and harmony is practically unthinkable without a change in human nature. And this is not an unrealistic hope, since it is already ten or so millennia since the epochal change when humans began to cultivate the land and so brought in civilisation. Such a change may indeed be on the way, if a sufficiently dynamic minority arises composed of people like ourselves, who accept necessary changes in our personal lives while maintaining our vision – a minority no more numerous than the relatively few humans who first began wearing clothes, settling in villages and eventually cities.

Marx and Nietzsche shaped the intellectual climate for the century now ending, and enhanced the powers of evil for wreaking massacre and destruction on a scale never known before. With the future of the habitat now in jeopardy, who is to shape the mental and cultural climate for the century and millennium which are coming? In this perspective the contribution of China, the living instance of continuity in a civilisation since civilisation began, may be decisive. As Confucius said, 'my way has one string which threads all together'.[7]

1.K.N.Walz: *Man, the State and War,* (Columbia University Press, New York and London 1959),14.
2.Ibid.,40.
3.Idem.
4.Ibid.,238.
5.*Power Politics*,214-5.
6.Ibid.,168*ff.*
7.Hughes, op.cit.,13.

INDEX

211

215

221

The maps and charts which follow were produced by the Drawing Office of the Royal Naval College, Greenwich.

EXPANSION OF THE AREA OF CIVILISATION, 3,000 B.C. ONWARDS

CHINA
(SHANG)
ANYANG

FERTILE
CRESCENT

AKKAD
(BABYLONIAN)
SUMER

INDUS HARAPPA
MOHENJO-
DARO

CRETE
(MINOAN)
EGYPT
(OLD KINGDOM)

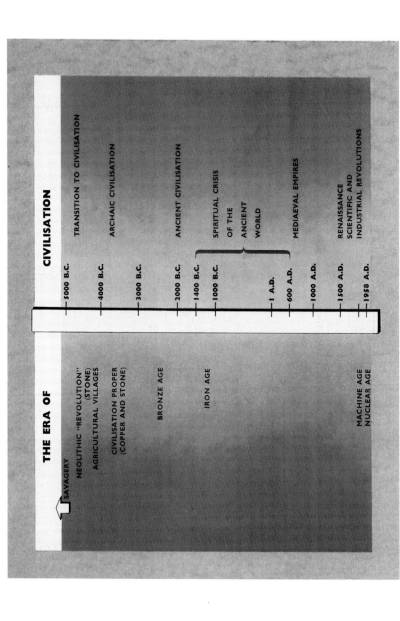

THE ERA OF CIVILISATION

SAVAGERY

NEOLITHIC "REVOLUTION" (STONE)
AGRICULTURAL VILLAGES

CIVILISATION PROPER
(COPPER AND STONE)

BRONZE AGE

IRON AGE

MACHINE AGE
NUCLEAR AGE

CIVILISATION

5000 B.C. — TRANSITION TO CIVILISATION

4000 B.C. — ARCHAIC CIVILISATION

3000 B.C. —

2000 B.C. — ANCIENT CIVILISATION

1400 B.C. — SPIRITUAL CRISIS
1000 B.C. — OF THE
            ANCIENT
            WORLD

1 A.D. —

600 A.D. — MEDIAEVAL EMPIRES

1000 A.D. —

1500 A.D. — RENAISSANCE
            SCIENTIFIC AND
1958 A.D. — INDUSTRIAL REVOLUTIONS

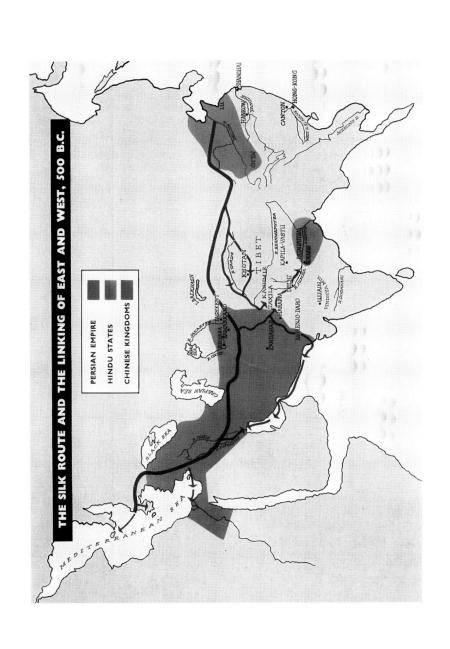

THE SILK ROUTE AND THE LINKING OF EAST AND WEST, 500 B.C.

PERSIAN EMPIRE
HINDU STATES
CHINESE KINGDOMS

MOSLEM CONQUEST AND THE MEDIAEVAL EQUILIBRIUM, C. 1000 A.D.